A KANJI STROKE ORDER MANUAL

FOR HEART SUTRA COPYING

Nadja Van Ghelue

I dedicate this book to my father and mother.

A Kanji Stroke Order Manual for Heart Sutra Copying

Copying a sutra text, known as shakyo in Japanese, is my own way of deepening my understanding of the Dharma teachings.

Those of you who are familiar with my website and art work know that many of my calligraphies are inspired by the Prajnaparamita Heart Sutra teachings of the Buddhist wisdom tradition and that copying the Heart Sutra is a calligraphic practice that is central to my art work.

A few years ago I made an artistic copy of the Heart Sutra in *tensho*, seal script, which was published as *The Heart Sutra in Calligraphy: A Visual Appreciation of the Perfection of Wisdom*. In this book I encourage the reader to copy the Heart Sutra in the enigmatic seal script.

This time I have brushed the Heart Sutra in *kaisho* or regular script and I would like to introduce you to the practice of Heart Sutra copying in *kaisho*. First, *A Kanji Stroke Order Manual for Heart Sutra Copying* is meant for beginners of Japanese calligraphy who want to study the Heart Sutra and perfect their calligraphic skills by means of Heart Sutra copying. Secondly, it is also and especially dedicated to all Dharma Zen students who are familiar with the Heart Sutra text and want to practice sutra copying as a form of meditation in action, copying the Japanese characters or kanji of the Heart Sutra with a brush pen, ballpoint, or any other kind of pen.

The core of this manual is my own copy of the Heart Sutra in kaisho in large-sized characters through which I show you the stroke order for each of the 276 kanji of the Heart Sutra. Knowing the stroke order for each kanji is the major key to calm sutra copying. Next to the calligraphies you will also find a table with the romaji or romanized form of the kanji and a word for word translation into English. Where the Japanese is a transliteration of the Sanskrit, I have given the original Sanskrit word.

The Heart Sutra, A Companion

I started learning Japanese calligraphy by means of the Heart Sutra. Actually, my first attempt to brush kanji was copying the Heart Sutra in regular script. I was neither acquainted with Japanese nor with Buddhism. But as it happens in life, suddenly I found myself practicing shodo, the way of the brush, and studying Dharma, the teaching of the Buddha. Since then the Heart Sutra has been my calligraphy teacher. Slowly but steadily copying the Heart Sutra, I have improved my calligraphic skills and deepened my knowledge of the emptiness teachings of the Heart Sutra. The Heart Sutra has become my companion in my search for wisdom and artistic inspiration.

This is why I decided to write this book with my own copy of the Heart Sutra in regular script with the explanation of the stroke order, the romaji and translation of the 276 kanji of the Heart Sutra; to pass on my experience and to provide you with a practicable self-study reference manual for Heart Sutra shakyo in regular script.

Copying of the Heart Sutra in Kanji for Westerners

Perhaps you are already familiar with the traditional Buddhist Japanese or Chinese Heart Sutra tracing papers. They feature the Heart Sutra faintly printed on a single sheet, usually in small kaisho, where you trace the characters with a brush or pen. They are very practical, often beautifully printed on ornamental sutra papers and induce a devotional copy practice. This is one way of copying the Heart Sutra.

For many Westerners the fact that these tracing papers show the characters in small kaisho, sometimes not larger than 0.6 in (1,5 cm), frustrates any attempt to copy the Heart Sutra in kanji.

Therefore in this Heart Sutra copying manual I suggest you copy the Heart Sutra in the same way as I was introduced to it, as if you were learning Japanese calligraphy. You brush the characters from scratch and copy them in large regular script, large size characters, more or less the same size as in this book: about 2 to 2.5 in (5 to 7 cm).

The Kanji Stroke Order

What is meant by the stroke order of a kanji and why is it important to know it?

The stroke order of a kanji is a fixed sequence in which the strokes and dots of a character are written. If you know the stroke order of a Japanese character it is easier to write it, it helps you to structure and balance the kanji more effortlessly.

Consider the given stroke order in this book not as a restrictive set of rules but as an aid, so that even with little or no knowledge of Japanese characters, you can start copying the Heart Sutra. Let's say you have the map for each character and the road is clear. This manual provides each kanji with its stroke order and you only have to follow it. In so doing you can copy with more ease.

I have followed the standard stroke order for kanji of modern Japan as the general stroke order reference framework. Nevertheless, sometimes you might find a variant stroke order. Please don't make a fuss of it. The stroke order in kaisho is fixed, but at the same time it is organic in such a way that each calligrapher has his/her own preferences. This being my own hand-brushed copy of the Heart Sutra it has my own mark.

The Honest Brush in Expressive Kaisho

In my search for copies of the Heart Sutra in kaisho, I came across an original brushed by the Chinese calligrapher Liu Kung-ch'üan (Liu Gongquan, 778-865), one of the late T'ang calligraphers. His Heart Sutra inspired the copy I brushed for this Heart Sutra shakyo manual.

Why Liu Kung-ch'üan? Liu Kung-ch'üan was born in the T'ang dynasty (618 - 907) the most crucial and innovating period for regular script. Four T'ang calligraphers stand out: Ou-yang Hsün (Ouyang Xun), Yü Shih-nan (Yu Shinan), Ch'u Sui-liang (Chu Suiliang), and Yen Chen-ch'ing (Yan Zhenqing). They were the masters who developed and established the traditional form and brush technique for regular script as we know it today.

Notorious in this dynamic calligraphic context is Yen Chen-ch'ing (709-785). He turned his back to the esthetic conventions of his time, which until then had been dominated by the style of Wang Hsi-chih (Wang Xizhi), the 4th century Chinese calligraphy sage. Wang Hsi-chih's calligraphy represents elegance, gracefulness, and refinement. Yen Chen-ch'ing broke completely with this centuries-old Chinese calligraphy tradition and deliberately shaped a forceful, for his time even an awkward kaisho style. Terms that are often applied to describe his style are opulent and robust, powerful, vigorous, monumental, and dignified.

In my own terms I would say that Yen Chen-ch'ing developed a Zen-like expressive kaisho, with a revolutionary straightforwardness. It is this quality that strikes me most in his work, his truthfulness. Yen Chen-ch'ing wielded a generous **honest brush**, without paying too much attention neither to unnecessary details of style nor technique.

Although he never admitted whether he had studied Yen Chen-ch'ing, Liu Kung-ch'üan definitely modeled his style after Yen and especially inherited his honest brush. Because of those two exceptional qualities, being a copy of the T'ang dynasty and having this straightforward spirit, I have chosen Liu Kung-ch'üan's Heart Sutra as the model for this manual.

My own idea of *copying* Liu Kung-ch'üan is not to *imitate* the style of Liu Kung-ch'üan merely in terms of outer similarity, but to catch his spirit and to inspire you with my own straightforward copy to wield a generous upright brush.

In this connection I would like to share the following anecdote with you. Liu Kung-ch'üan was the main calligraphy teacher at the imperial court for more than twenty years. One day the emperor asked him how he was always able to shape upright characters. Instead of giving technical instructions to the emperor, he answered that it was enough to have the right mind.

It might also interest you to know that Liu Kung-ch'üan was a devoted Buddhist. Besides the Heart Sutra he also left us a copy of the Vajracchedika Prajnaparamita Sutra, known in English as The Diamond Sutra, another gem for sutra copying.

Actual Sutra Copying

In what order should you copy the calligraphies on each page?

I have brushed the Heart Sutra in the traditional way of Chinese and Japanese calligraphy; vertically, in columns going from right to left. Thus, to copy the Heart Sutra, you start at page one, copy all kanji, from top to bottom and from right to left and then move to the next one, and so on.

Preliminaries

In this kanji stroke order manual for Heart Sutra copying I assume that you are acquainted with the required Japanese calligraphy supplies and know the basic technique and brushstrokes of Japanese calligraphy.

Set up your shakyo calligraphy table in a quiet, clean place where you can be on your own, undisturbed for at least one to one and a half hours.

I suggest the following calligraphy supplies: a medium-sized goat's hair brush about 0.35 x 1.49 in (0,9 x 3,8 cm), an ink stone, good quality liquid ink or a quality ink stick to grind ink, and rice paper.

If you are very new to Japanese calligraphy you might want to use single sheets of rice paper. If you make some major mistakes, you can easily do the page over again. As we will copy the characters more or less in the same size as shown in this book, namely characters of 2 to 2.5 in (5 to 7 cm) high, I suggest you fold the rice paper to approximately 3 in (8 cm) squares as a guide. Calculate any margins, if necessary, to have a proportional distribution of the kanji. Number the sheets so you keep the correct order.

For more experienced practitioners I recommend standard large sheets of Chinese Xuan paper (single layer) folded into squares of approximately 3 in (8 cm). A standard sheet of Chinese Xuan paper measures 27.56 x 54.33 in (70 x 138 cm). First fold the sheet lengthwise in two and then fold the sheet into approximately 3 in (8 cm) squares, leaving margins of 0.6 in (1,5 cm) above, below, right and left. You will need five of these folded sheets to copy the complete Heart Sutra.

If you are copying the Heart Sutra with a smaller Pentel brush or ball point pen, make sure you also have a set of sutra copying papers ready, in the same manner as I explained above, choosing the paper and size of the kanji that are appropriate for the brush or ball point you are using.

Heart Sutra Copying, A Creative Tool For Body and Mind Integration

Copying the Heart Sutra in large kaisho with the arm raised, not leaning on the table, is demanding, both physically and mentally, so you need to be very present. But this is what sutra copying as meditation is about, a way to harmonize body and mind. Genuine shakyo heightens your awareness; you become mentally less scattered and have more clarity of mind.

A few of the methods I mention hereafter help to support this body and mind integration.

Grind Your Ink

You will need a large amount of ink for this practice and it is fine to use good quality liquid ink for this purpose. Don't forget to add some water to bottled ink, as this ink tends to be stickier.

If you have time, grind your ink on the ink stone and prepare an amount of ink yourself. It quiets the mind and warms up your arm and hand. It has a synergetic and purifying effect; body and mind tune into your calligraphic performance. Moreover, when you grind a quality ink stick on your ink stone, it will diffuse the wonderful scent of resins, incense, and herbal ingredients that have been added to the ink. Grinding adds a sense of wholeness to your calligraphy space.

Introduce a Zen Meditation

Do a short Zen meditation before your shakyo session; apply a simple method, for instance counting the breath for five to ten minutes. This helps to calm down mentally and physically.

In the breathing meditation you concentrate on the area below the navel, the Hara, your physical and spiritual center. In Japanese calligraphy, on a deeper spiritual level, you draw your brush strokes from this vital center. Try to maintain this awareness during your shakyo session.

Visualize the Kanji

Visualization is a very important part of the Heart Sutra brush meditation.

The copy of the Heart Sutra lies in front of you. Look at the kanji(s) you are going to brush. Close your eyes and mentally conceive the kanji(s) you've looked at before. Use your index finger to "draw" the character(s) in the air, in accordance with the stroke order explained in this manual. Once the mind sees the image and the movement, you project the kanji(s) on the paper, *write* it with your index finger on the rice paper, and then actually brush it.

With this method you activate the body and mind integration in a very specific way. The clear image in the mind allows the body and the brush to respond effortlessly. In fact if you visualize well, the kanji(s) becomes more like a flowing movement, even in kaisho.

Formal Heart Sutra Shakyo Session

As you brush a copy of the Heart Sutra in large kaisho, you probably will need more than one session.

You sit at your calligraphy table and all is set up for the shakyo session; ink, brush and rice paper all is waiting.

The Heart Sutra manual lies open in front of you, at the page you are going to copy.

Bend slightly forward, bring the calligraphy brush to your forehead, and greet it.

Traditionally you now take refuge in the Three Jewels: the Buddha, the Dharma, and the Sangha.

Recite the Heart Sutra and do a short Zen meditation.

Visualize the kanji(s) you are going to copy and then brush each kanji slowly, with full awareness, one kanji after the other. Brush the characters with a straightforward mind.

Once you end your session, stay for a while within this calligraphic meditative state. Look in stillness at the copy you have just brushed, see without grasping or judging, just be aware and present.

Then dedicate all the merit produced by this sutra copying to all sentient beings, wishing that all beings may be freed from suffering and soon become awakened — Buddha.

Thunders and lightning
The windows slide and shut
Farewell says the hot summer

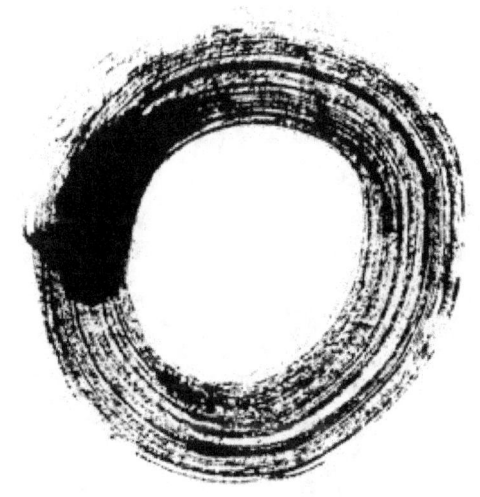

摩　MA　　　great

訶　KA

般　HAN

若　NYA　　prajnapara(mita)

波　HA

羅　RA

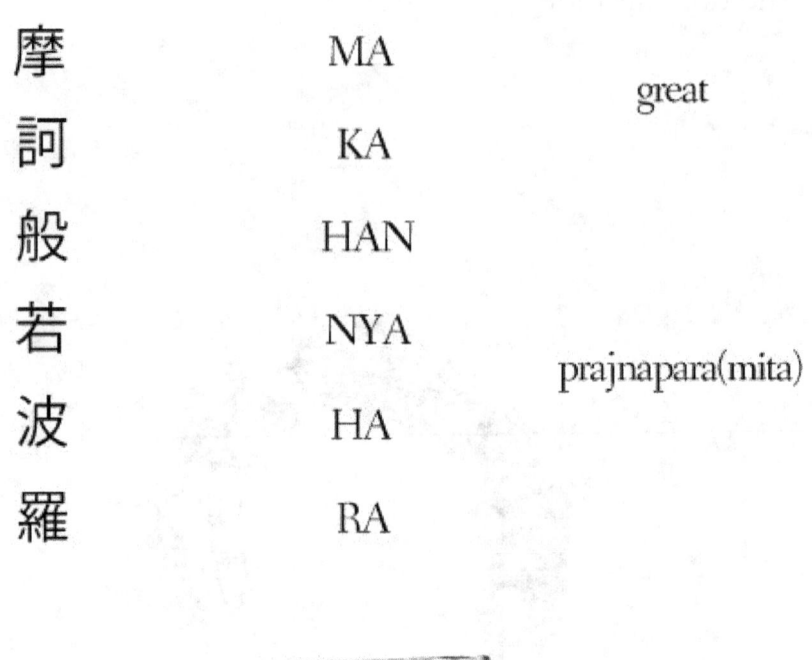

The Great Prajnaparamita Heart Sutra

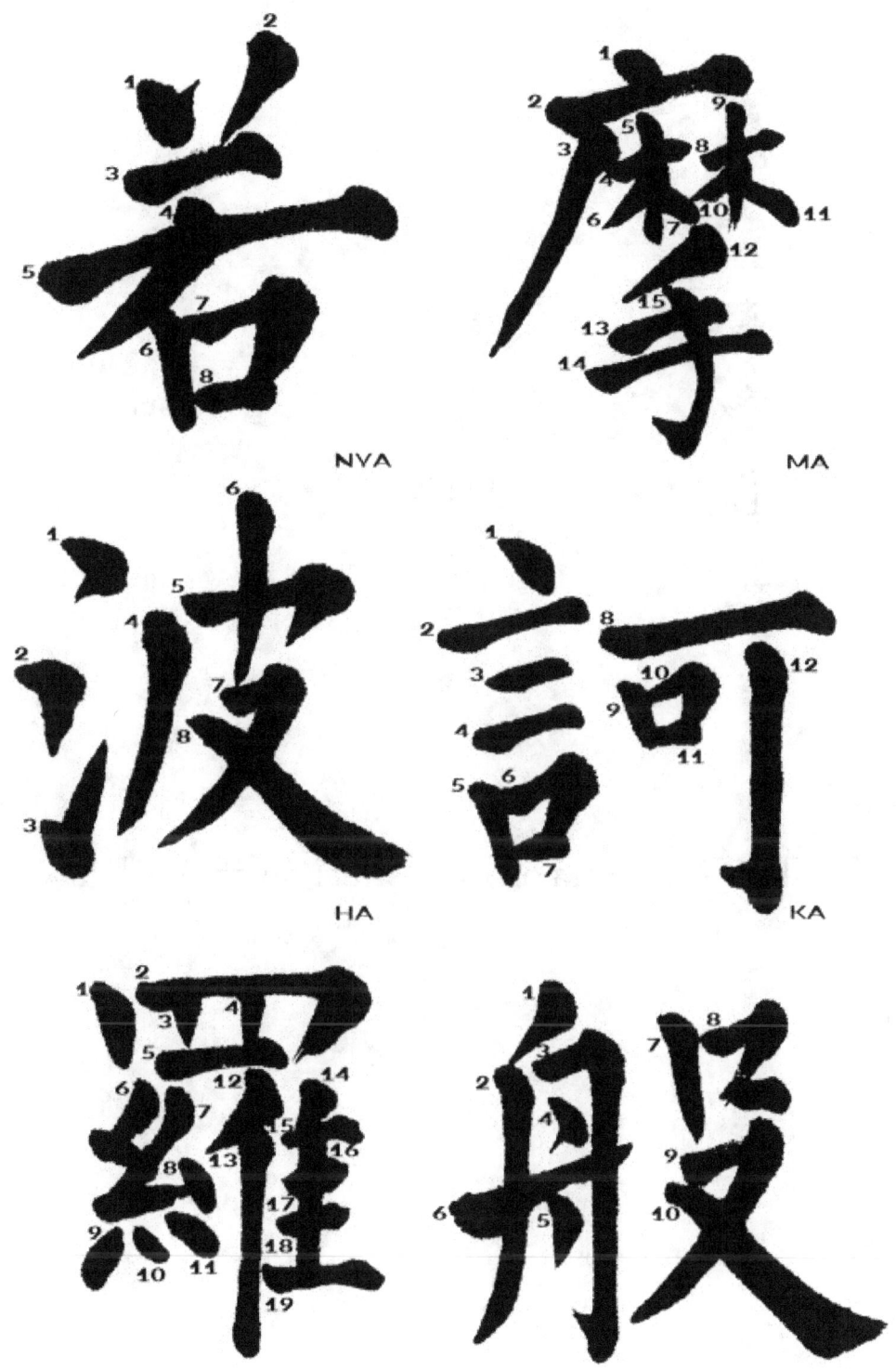

NYA

MA

HA

KA

RA

HAN

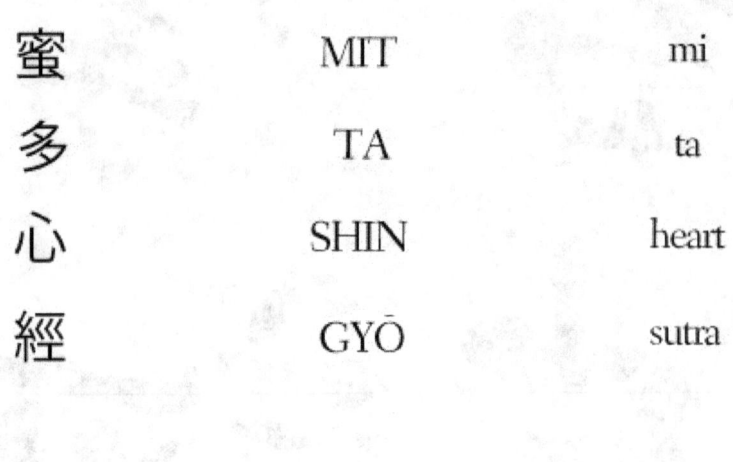

蜜	MIT	mi
多	TA	ta
心	SHIN	heart
經	GYŌ	sutra

The Heart Sutra on the Perfection of Wisdom

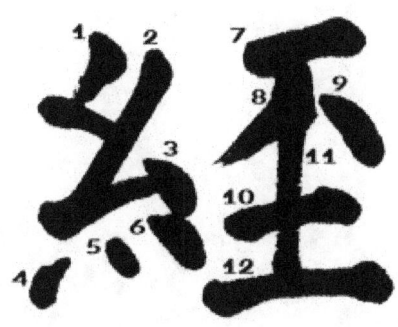

GYŌ

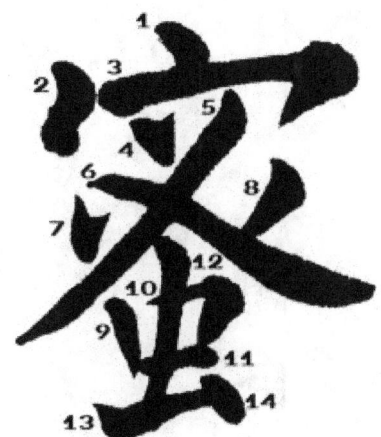

MIT

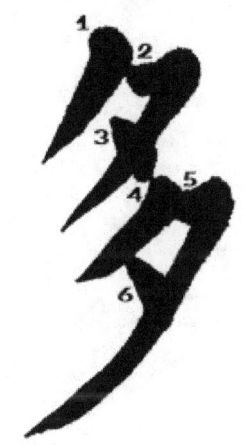

TA

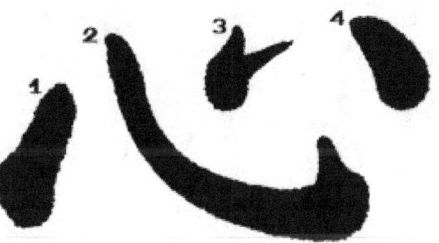

SHIN

觀	KAN	
自	JI	Avalokiteshvara
在	ZAI	
菩	BO	
薩	SATSU	bodhisattva
行	GYŌ	practice

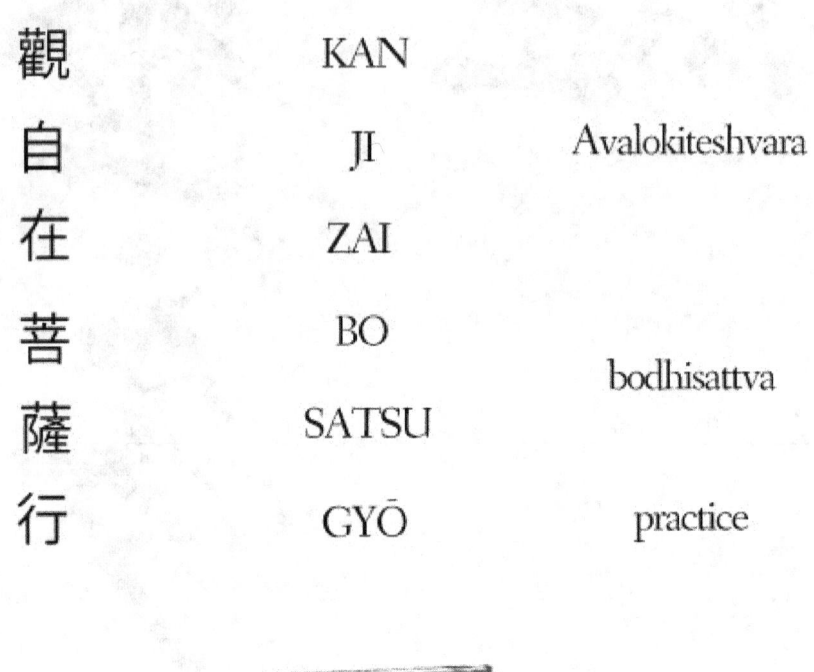

The Bodhisattva Avalokiteshvara,

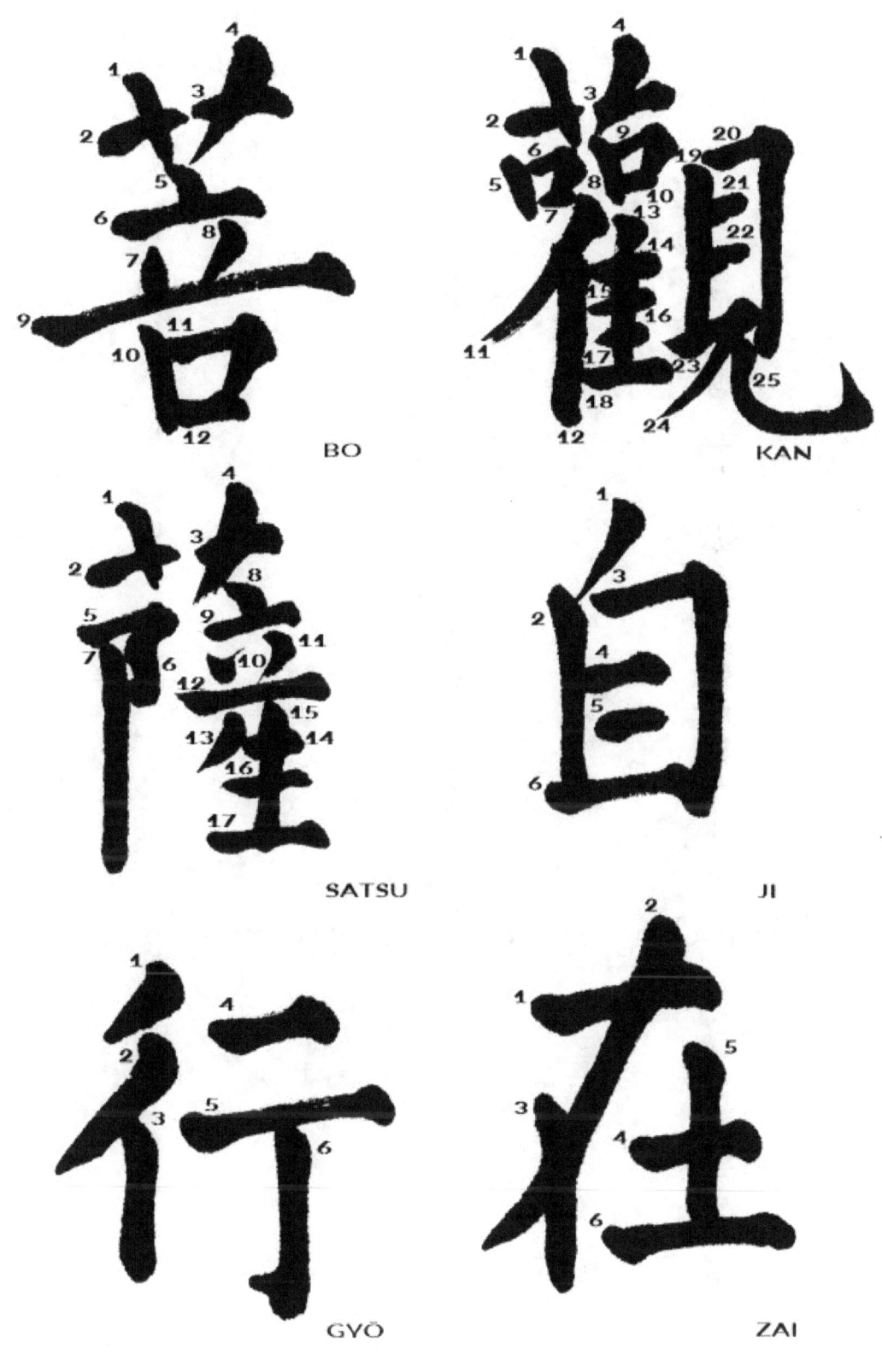

BO

KAN

SATSU

JI

GYŌ

ZAI

深	JIN	deep
般	HAN	
若	NYA	
波	HA	prajnaparami(ta)
羅	RA	
蜜	MIT	

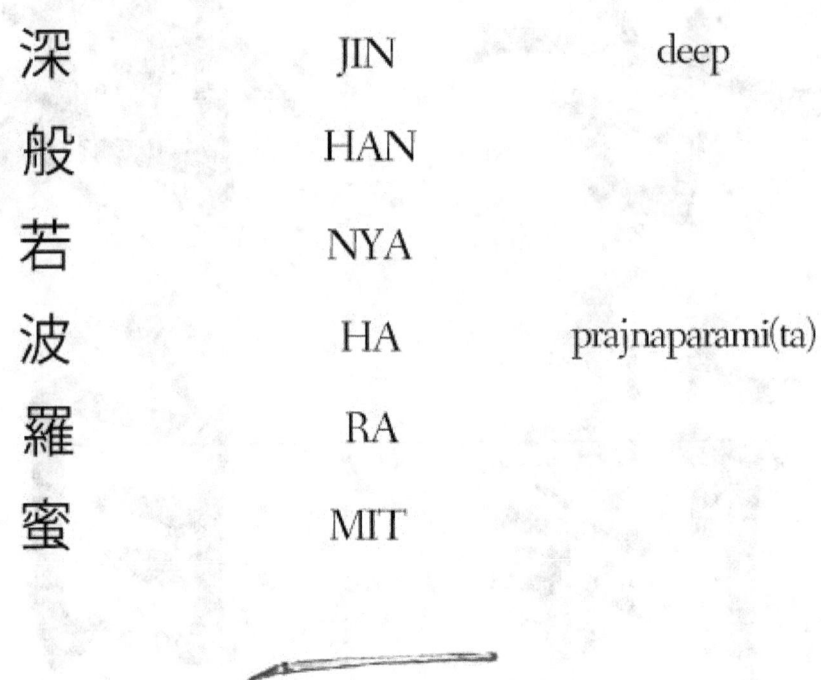

while dwelling in the deep practice of Prajnaparamita,

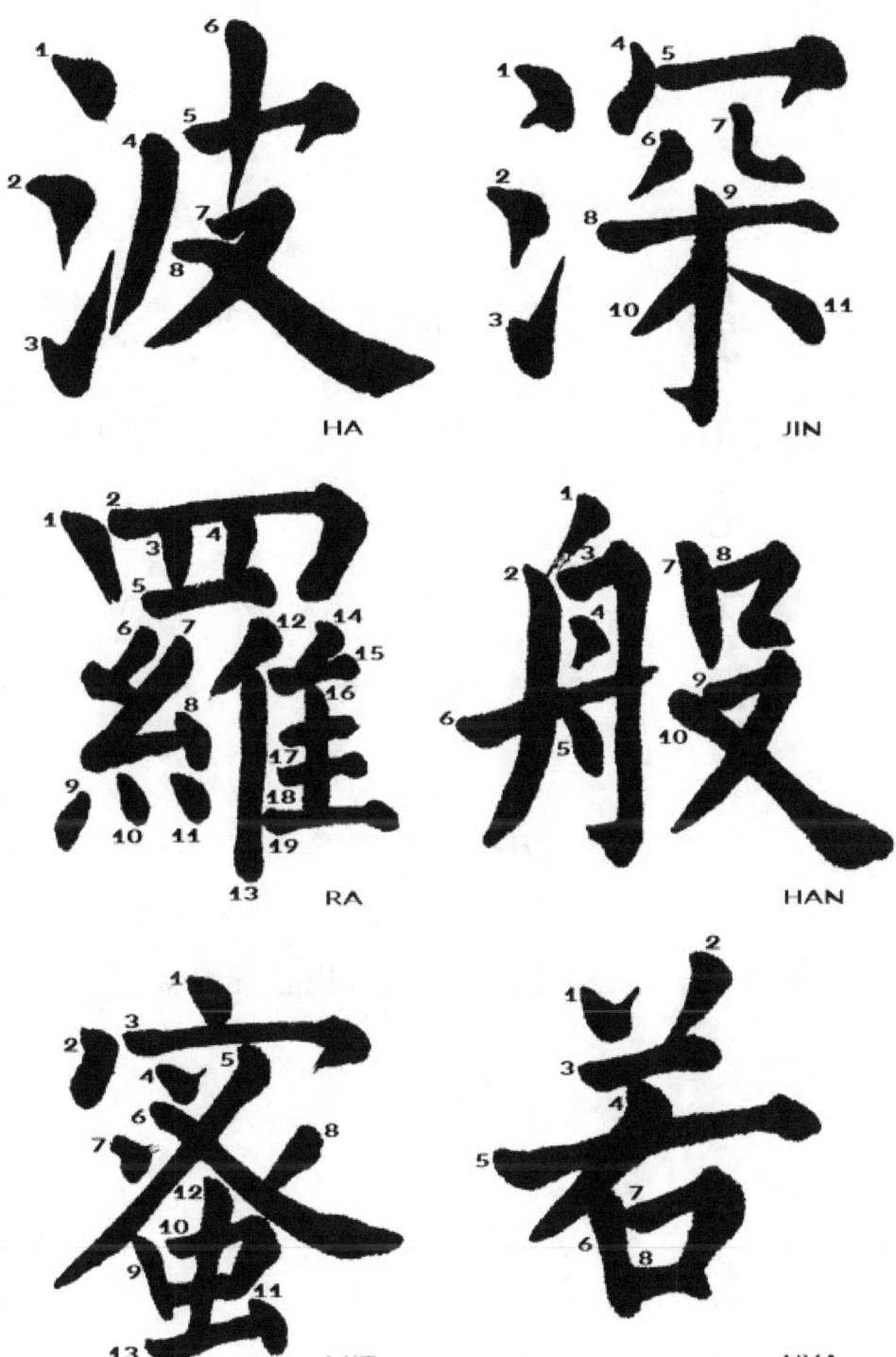

HA

JIN

RA

HAN

MIT

NVA

多時照見五蘊	TA	ta
	JI	when
	SHŌ	illuminate
	KEN	see
	GO	five
	UN	skandha

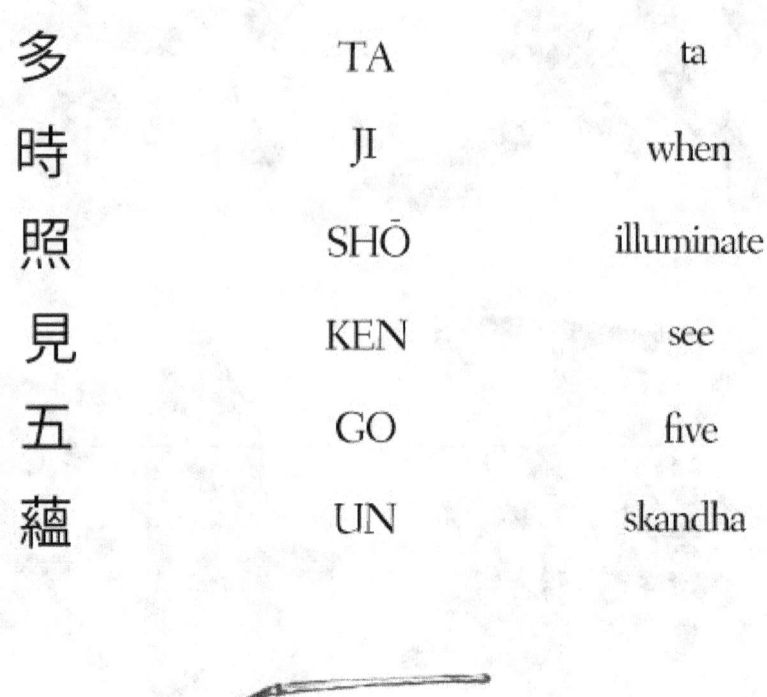

illuminated the five skandhas, and saw

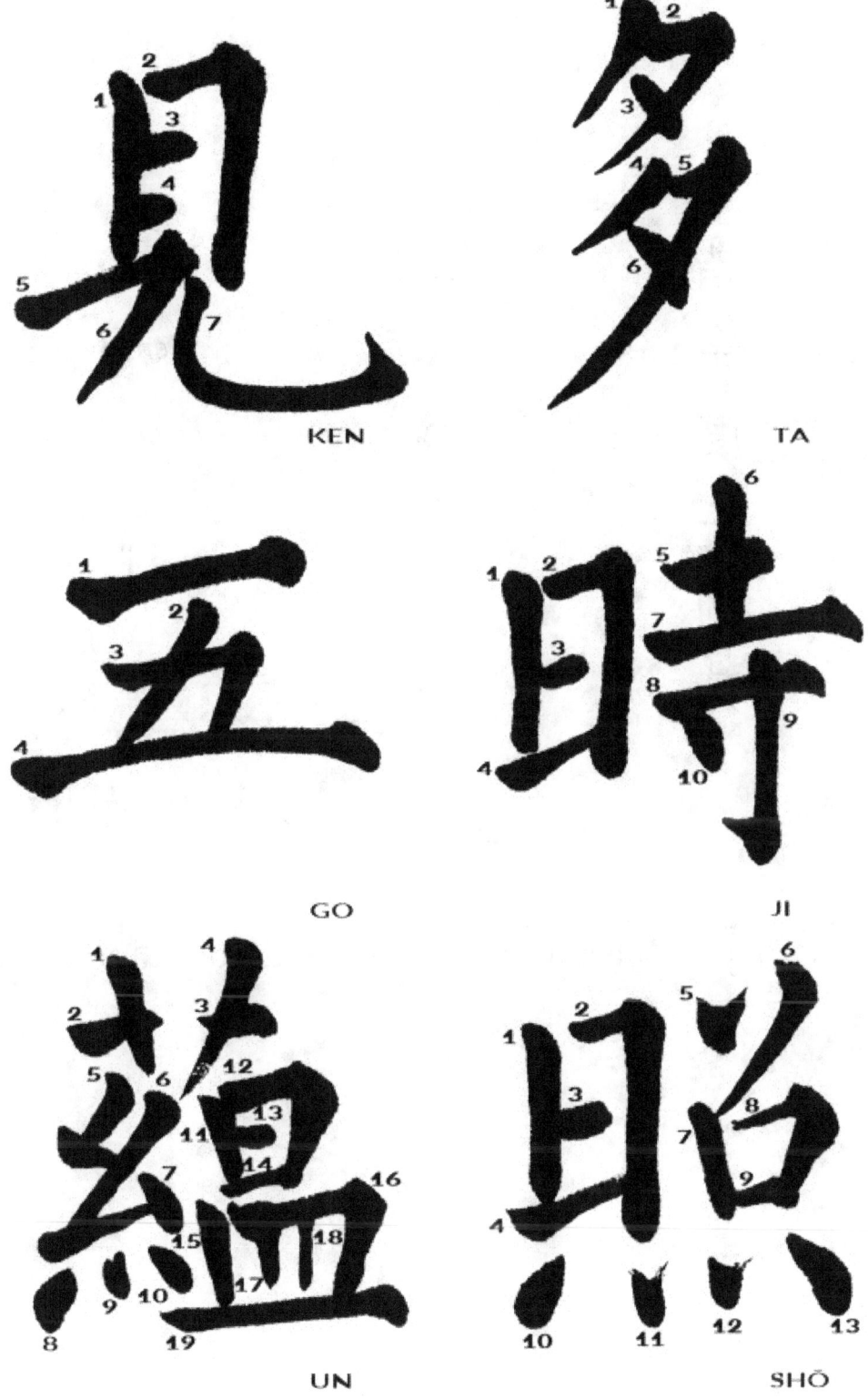

KEN

TA

GO

JI

UN

SHŌ

皆	KAI	all
空	KŪ	empty
度	DO	cross beyond
一	IS	all
切	SAI	
苦	KU	suffering

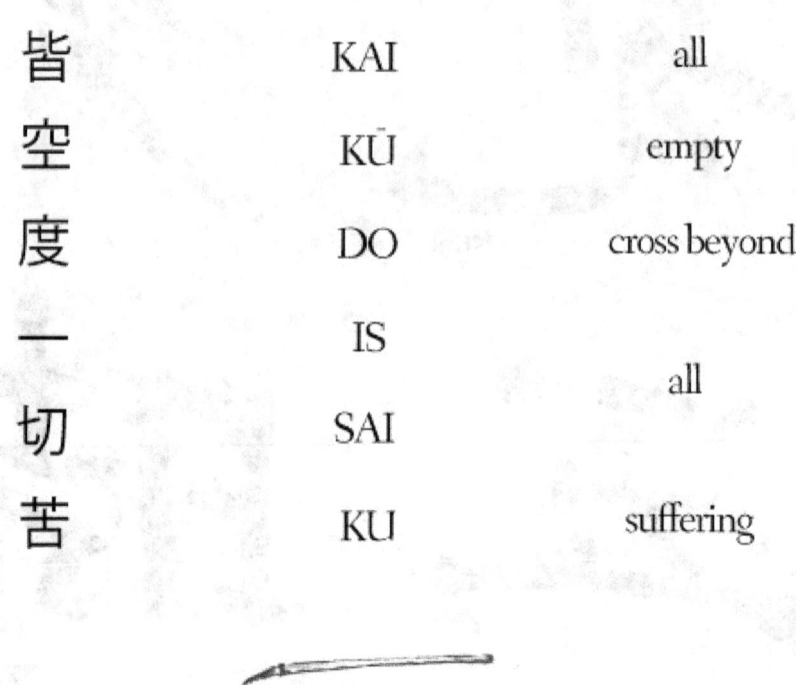

that they are all empty, and was freed from all suffering

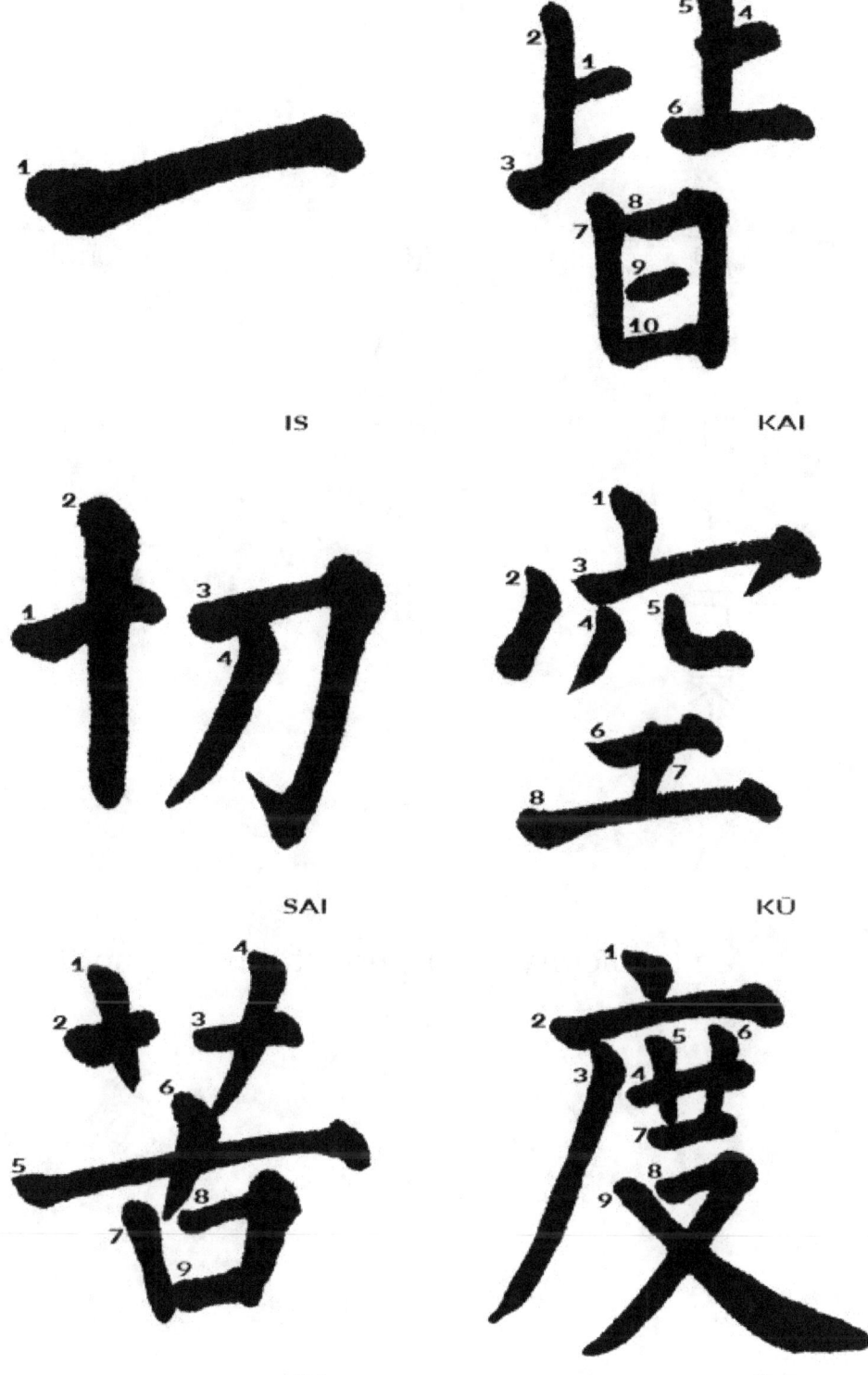

一 IS

皆 KAI

切 SAI

空 KŪ

苦 KU

度 DO

厄	YAKU	misfortune
舍	SHA	
利	RI	Shariputra
子	SHI	
色	SHIKI	form
不	FU	not

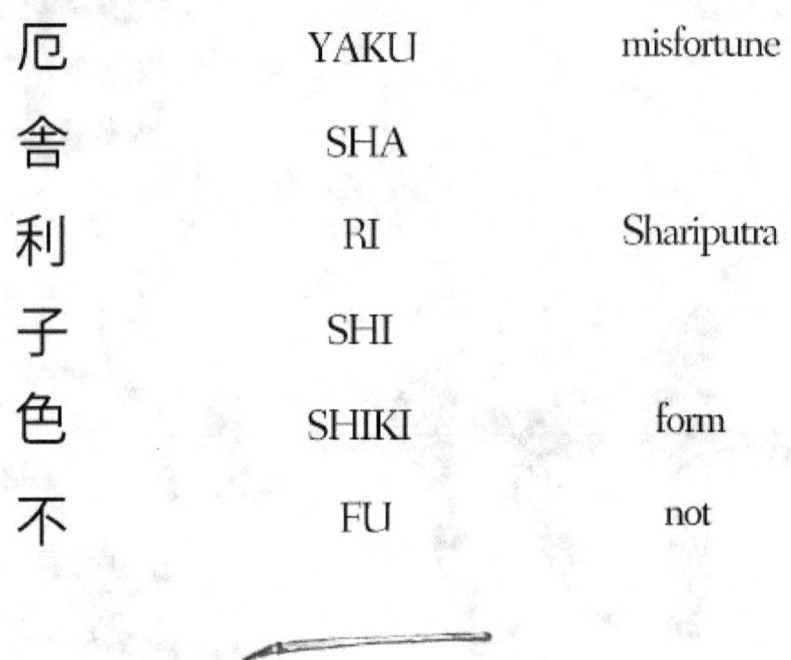

and difficulty. Shariputra, form does not

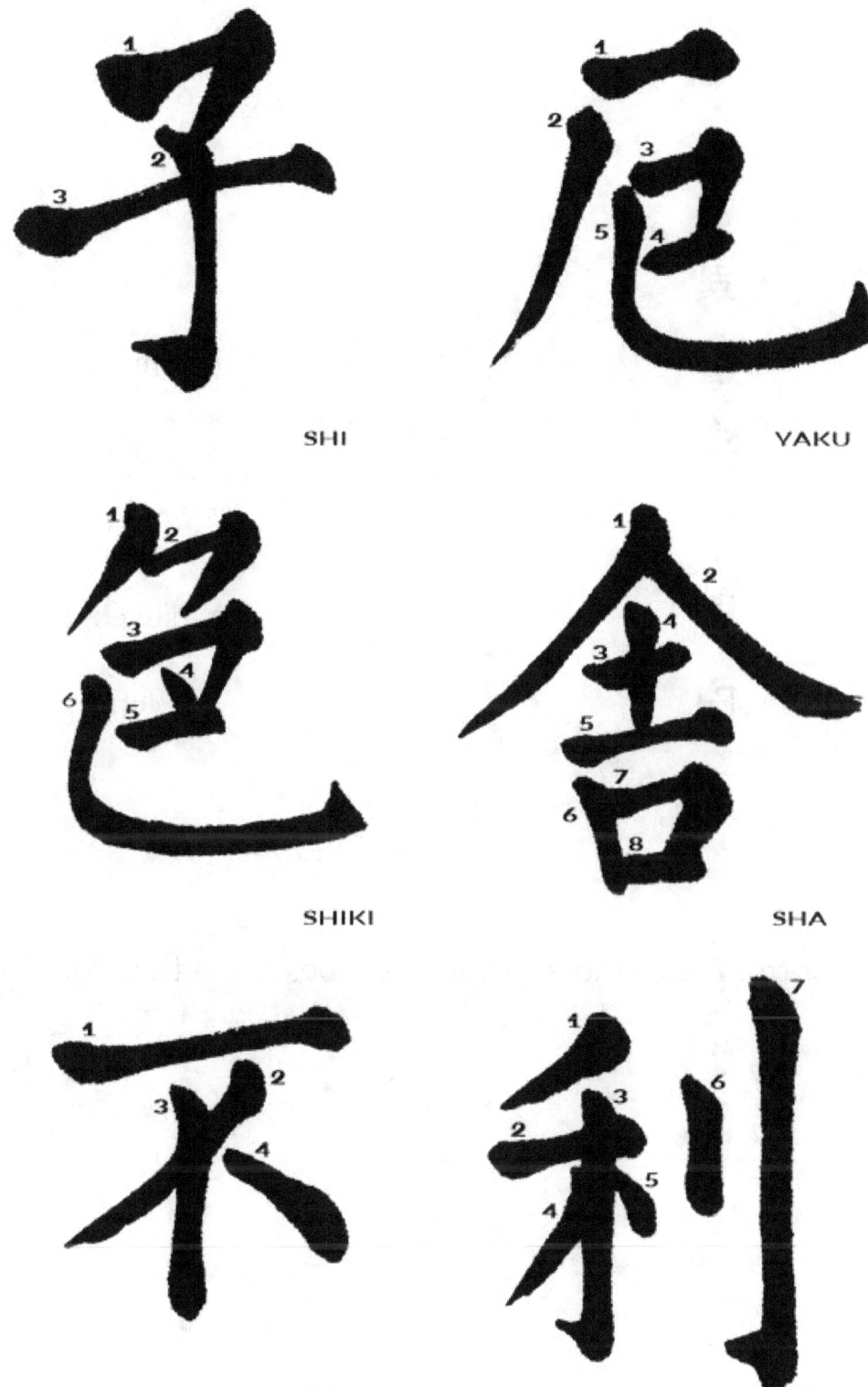

SHI

YAKU

SHIKI

SHA

FU

RI

異	I	differ from
空	KŪ	emptiness
空	KŪ	emptiness
不	FU	not
異	I	differ from
色	SHIKI	form

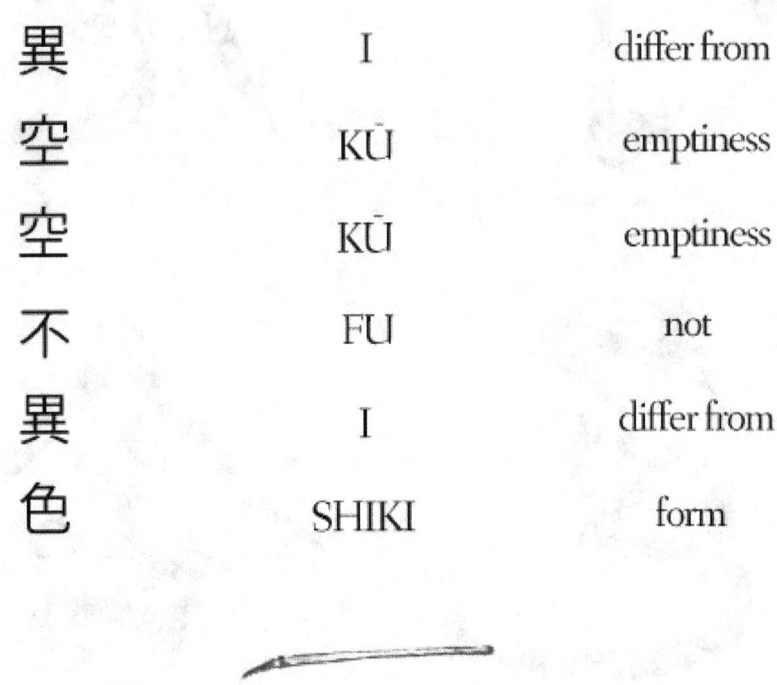

differ from emptiness, emptiness does not differ from form;

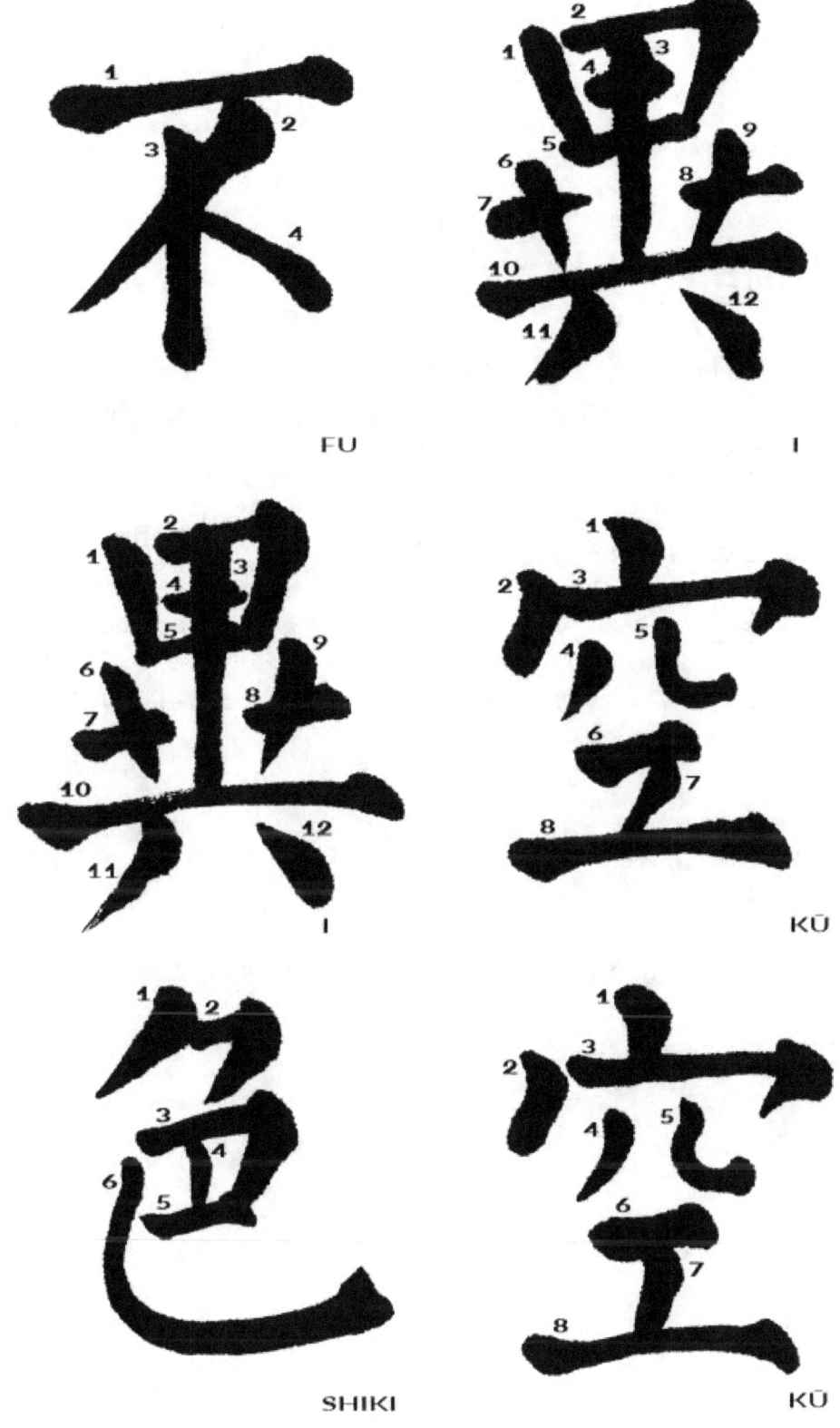

FU

I

I

KŪ

SHIKI

KŪ

色	SHIKI	form
即	SOKU	be identical
是	ZE	
空	KŪ	emptiness
空	KŪ	emptiness
即	SOKU	be identical

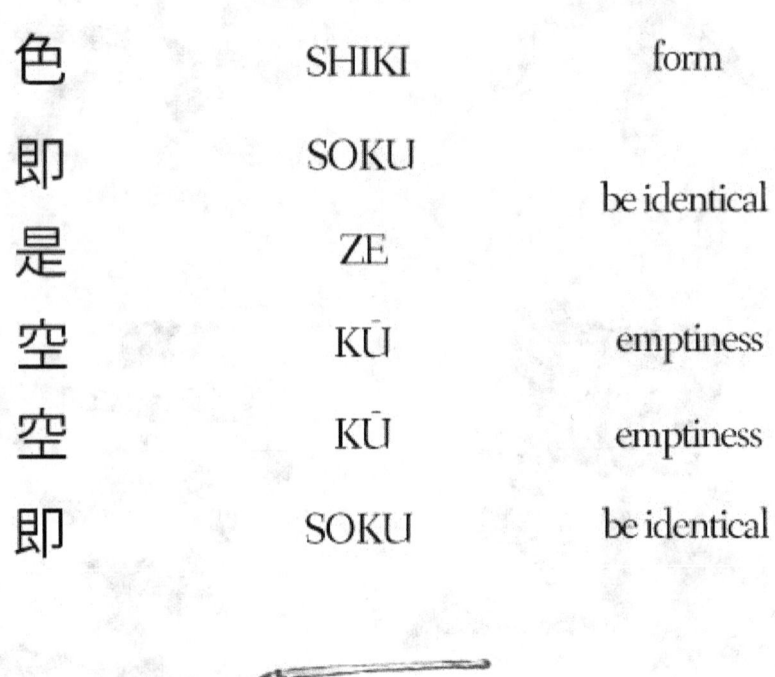

form is emptiness, emptiness is

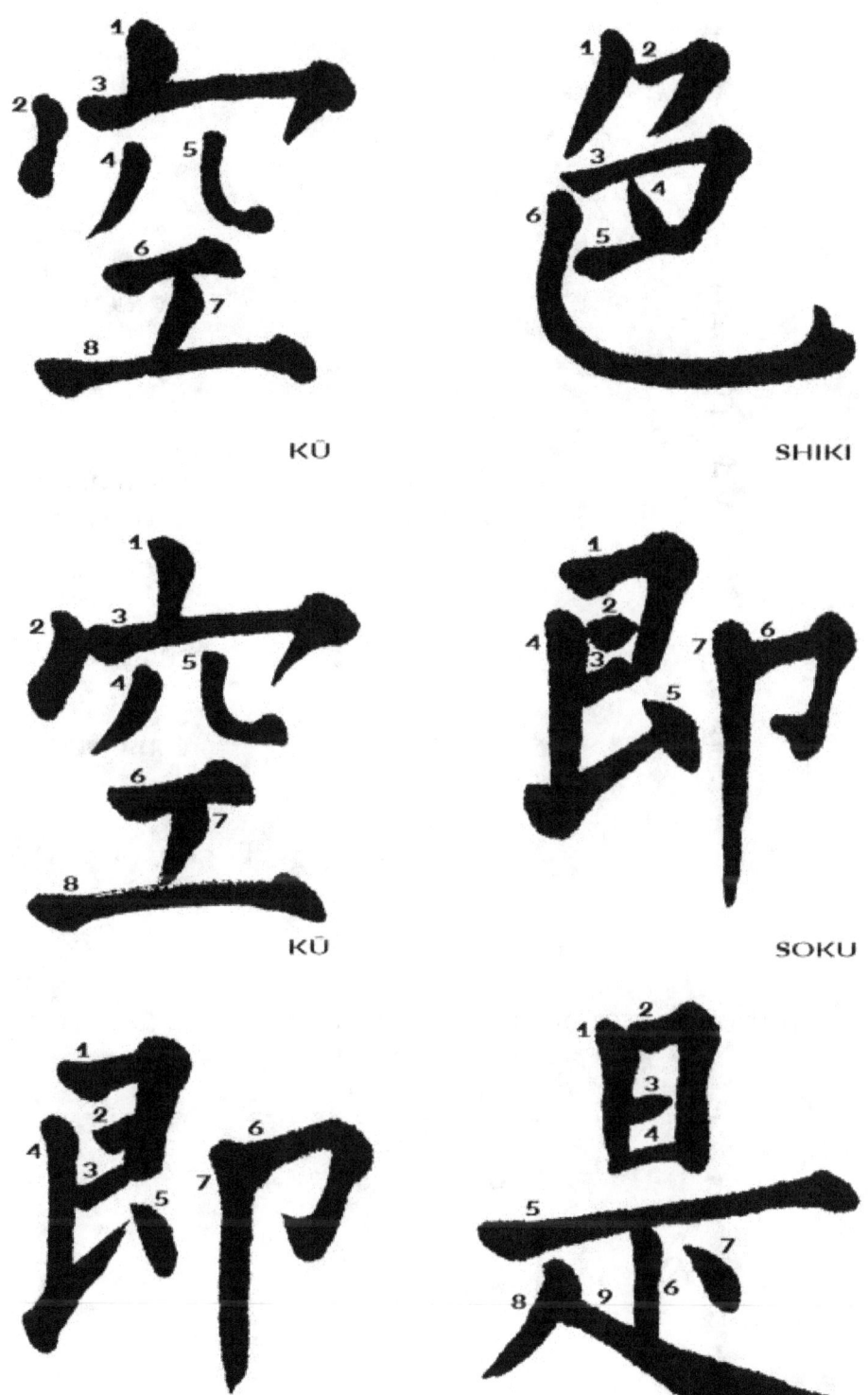

空
KŪ

色
SHIKI

空
KŪ

即
SOKU

即
SOKU

是
ZE

是	ZE	be identical
色	SHIKI	form
受	JU	sensation
想	SŌ	perception
行	GYŌ	mental formations
識	SHIKI	consciousness

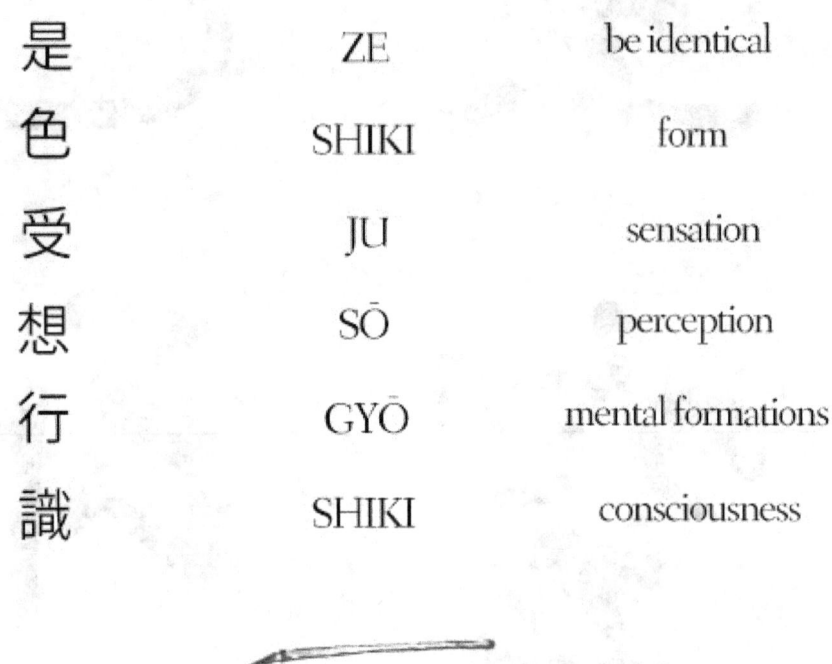

form. Sensation, perception, mental formations, and consciousness

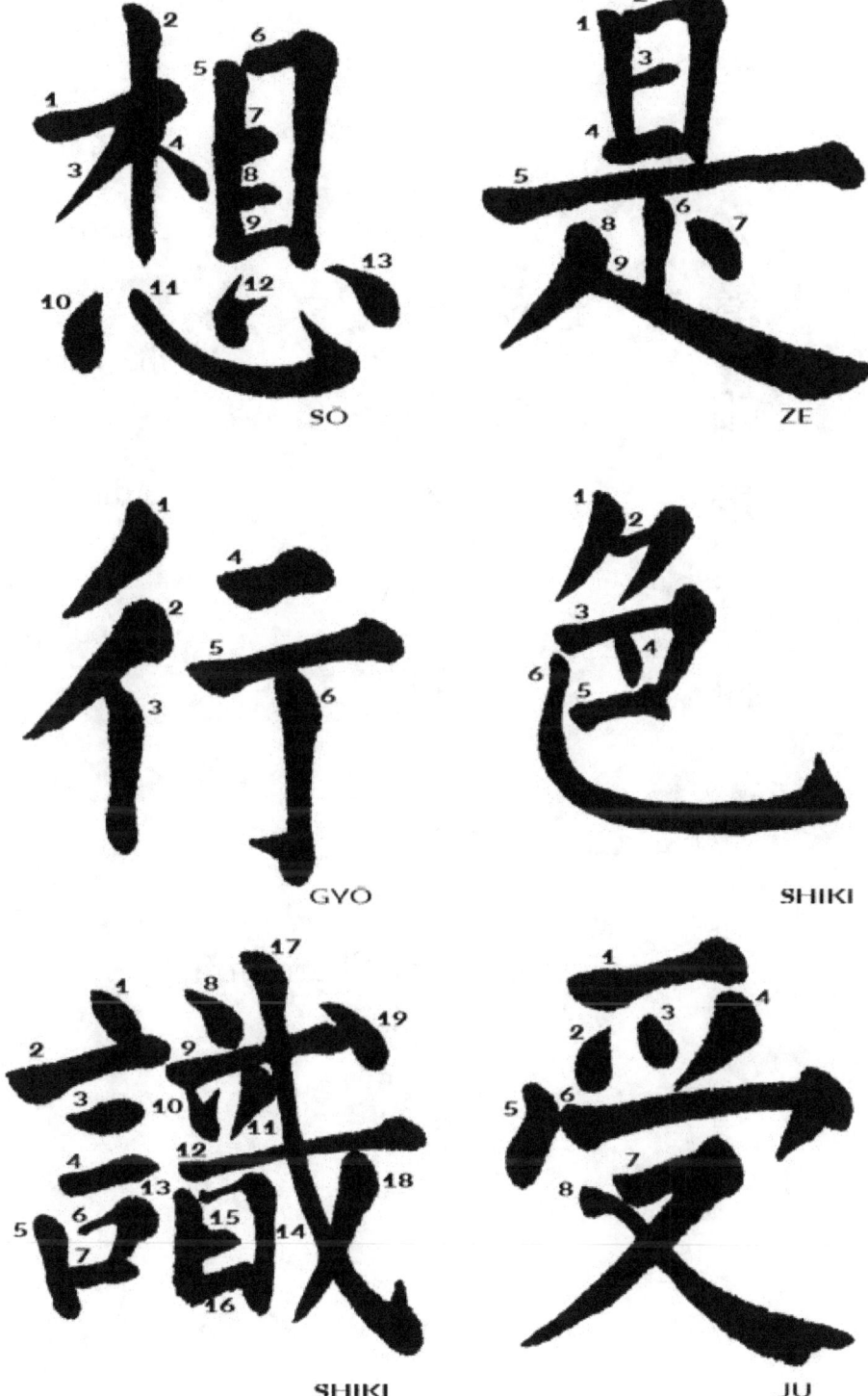

想 SŌ

是 ZE

行 GYŌ

色 SHIKI

識 SHIKI

受 JU

亦　YAKU　also

復　BU

如　NYO　be the same as

是　ZE　this

舎　SHA

利　RI　Shari(putra)

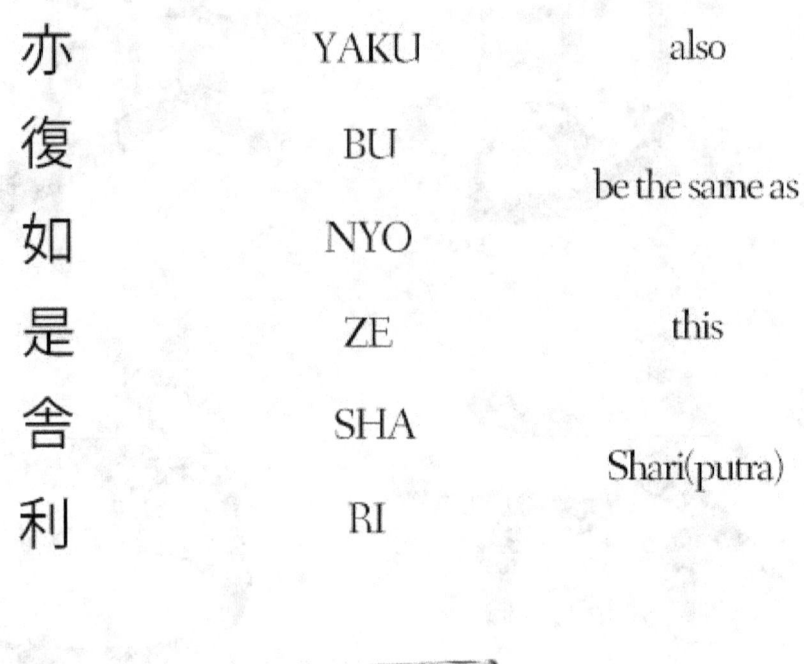

are also like this. Shariputra,

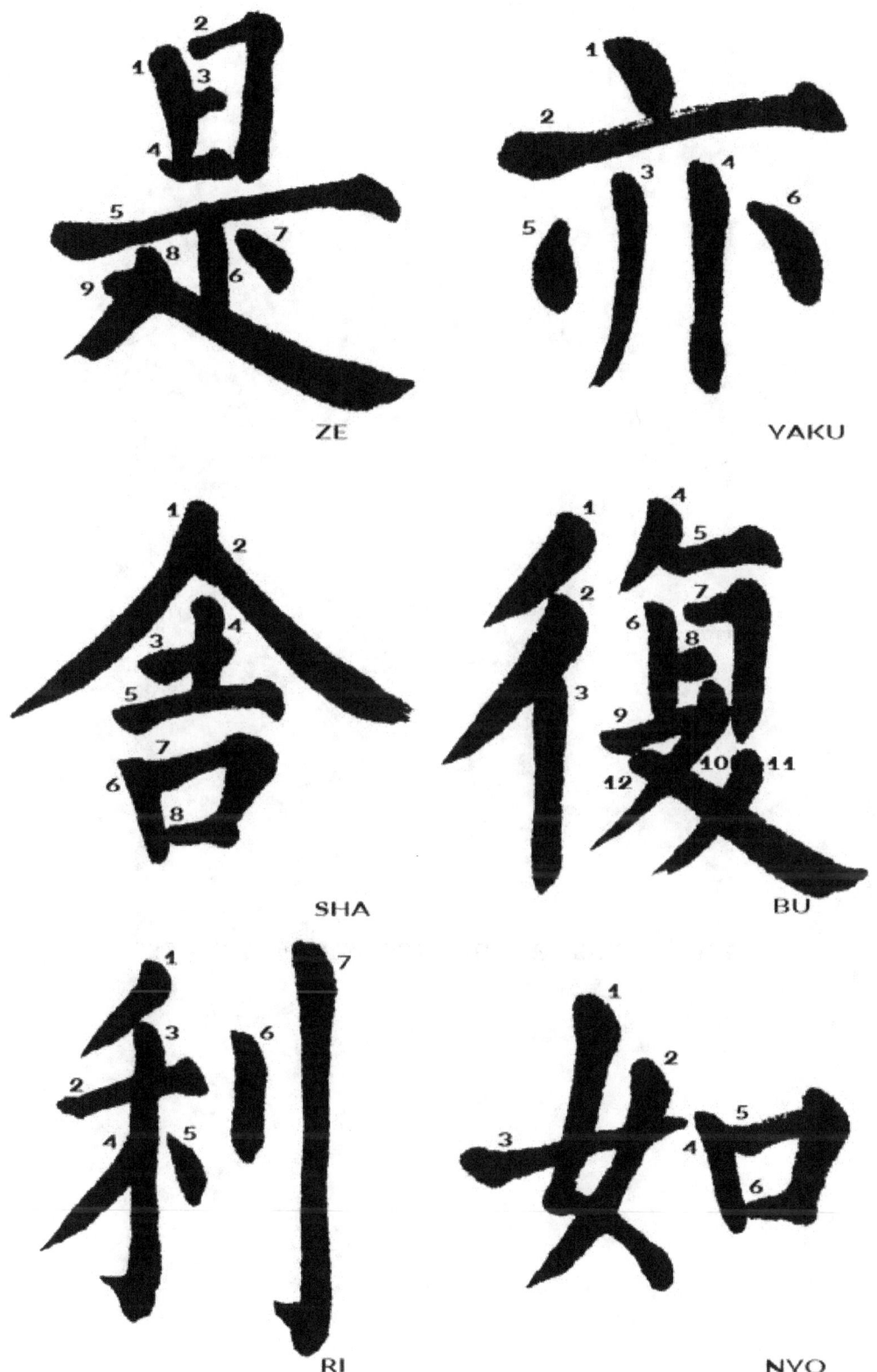

是 ZE

亦 YAKU

舍 SHA

復 BU

利 RI

如 NYO

子	SHI	putra
是	ZE	this
諸	SHO	all
法	HŌ	dharma
空	KŪ	emptiness
相	SŌ	mark

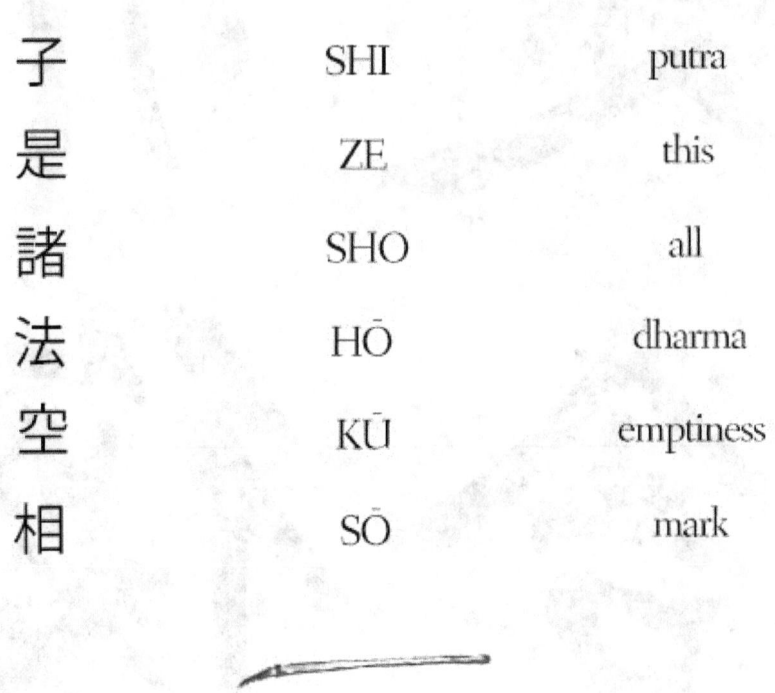

all dharmas are marked with emptiness;

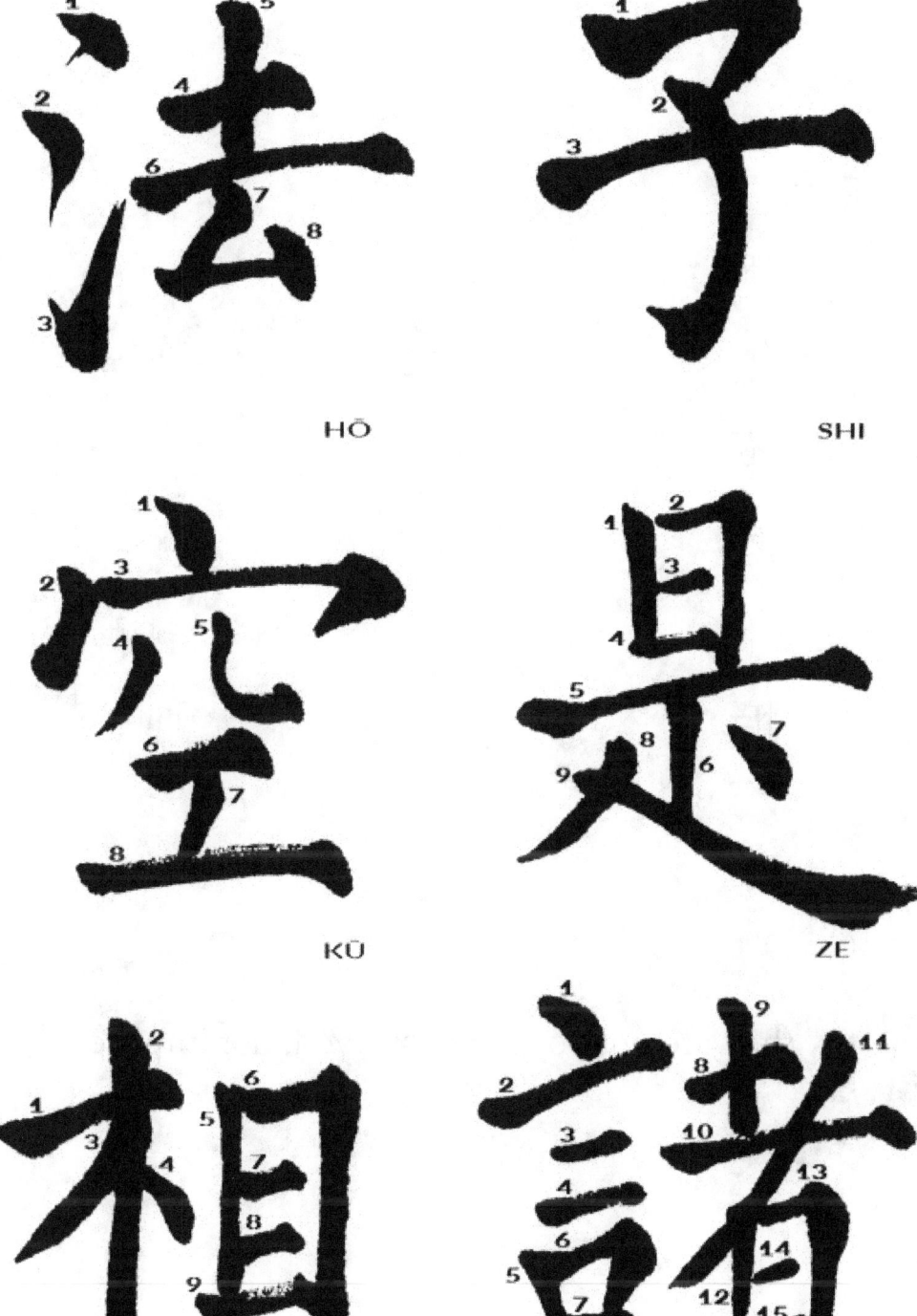

法 HŌ

子 SHI

空 KŪ

是 ZE

相 SŌ

諸 SHO

不	FU	not
生	SHŌ	born
不	FU	not
滅	METSU	destroy
不	FU	not
垢	KU	impure

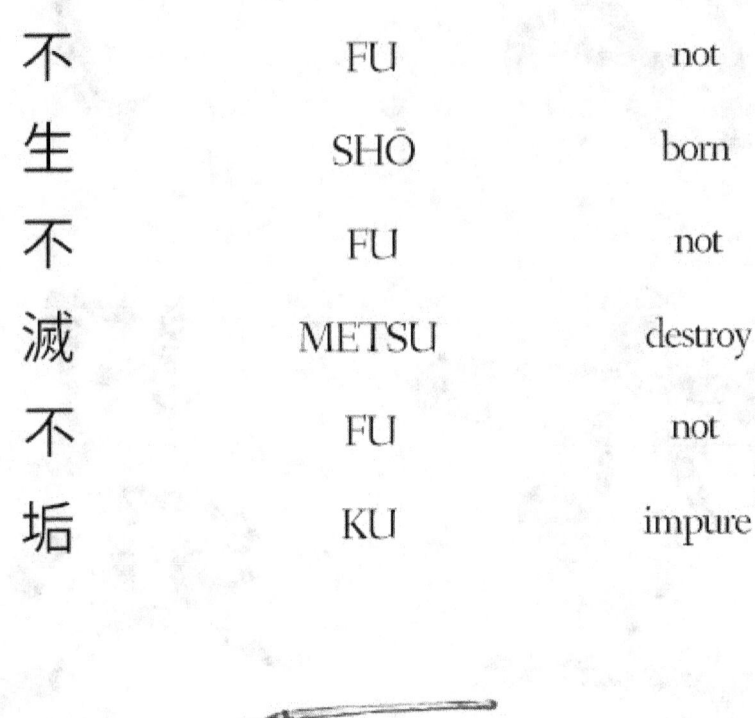

they are not born or destroyed, not impure

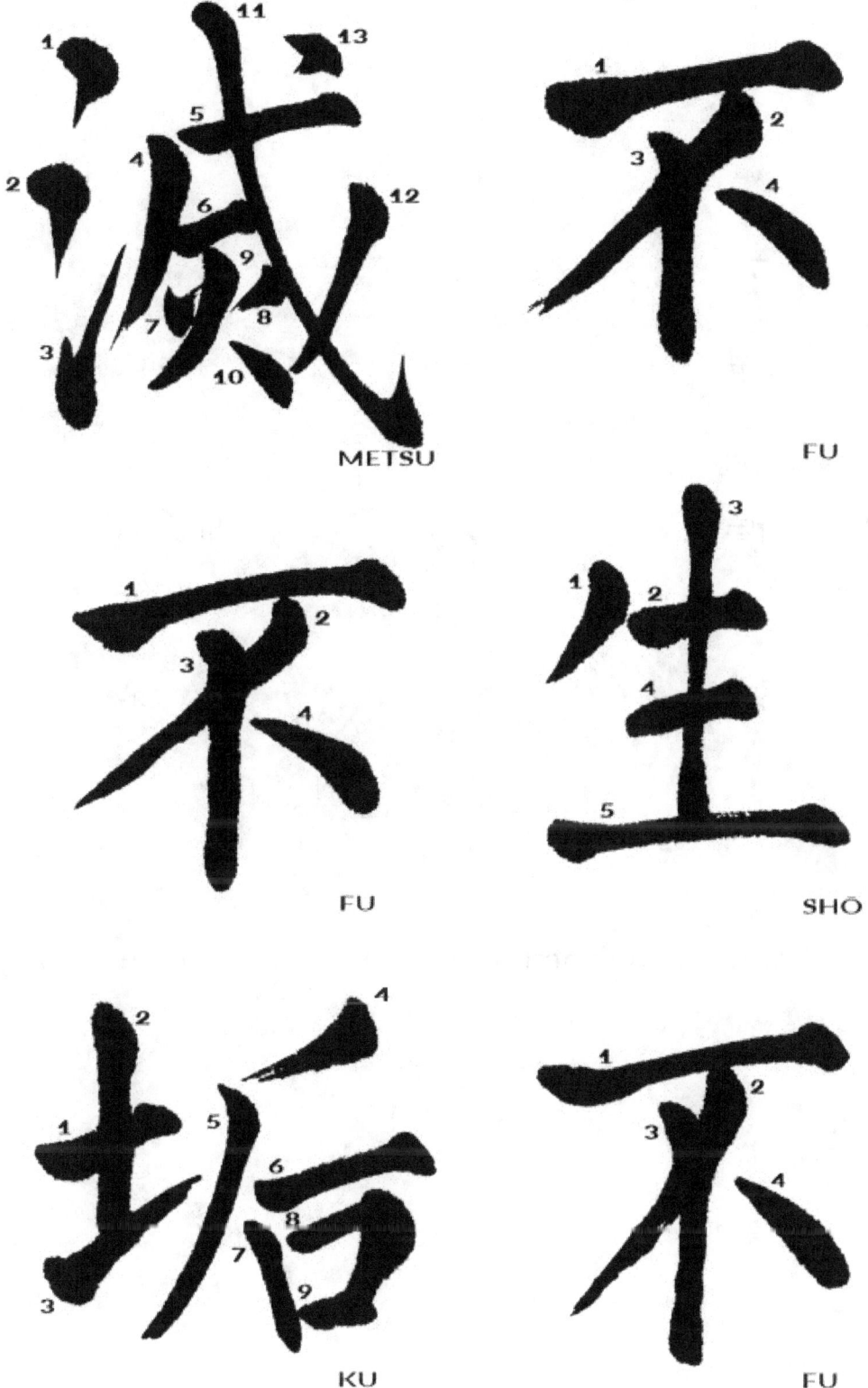

METSU

FU

FU

SHŌ

KU

FU

不	FU	not
淨	JŌ	pure
不	FU	not
增	ZŌ	increase
不	FU	not
減	GEN	decrease

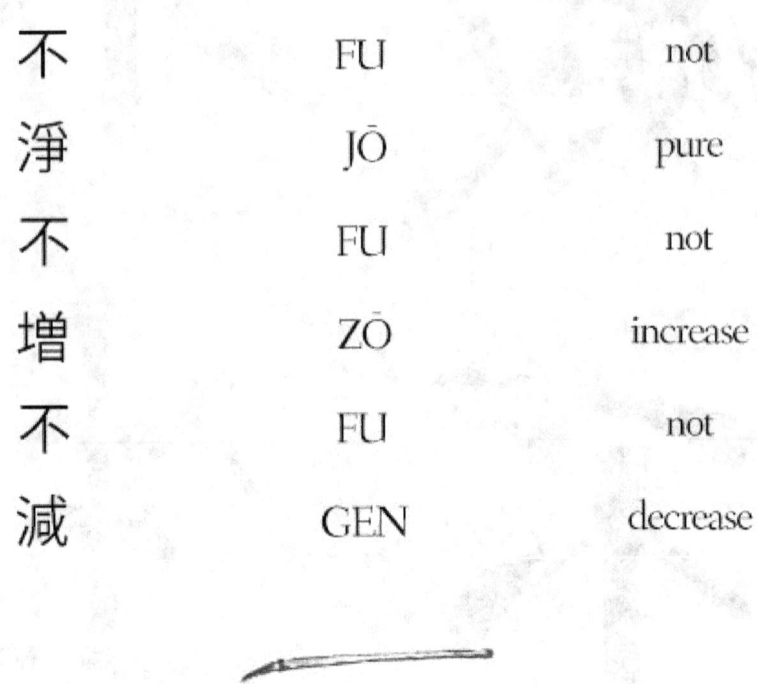

or pure, they neither increase nor decrease.

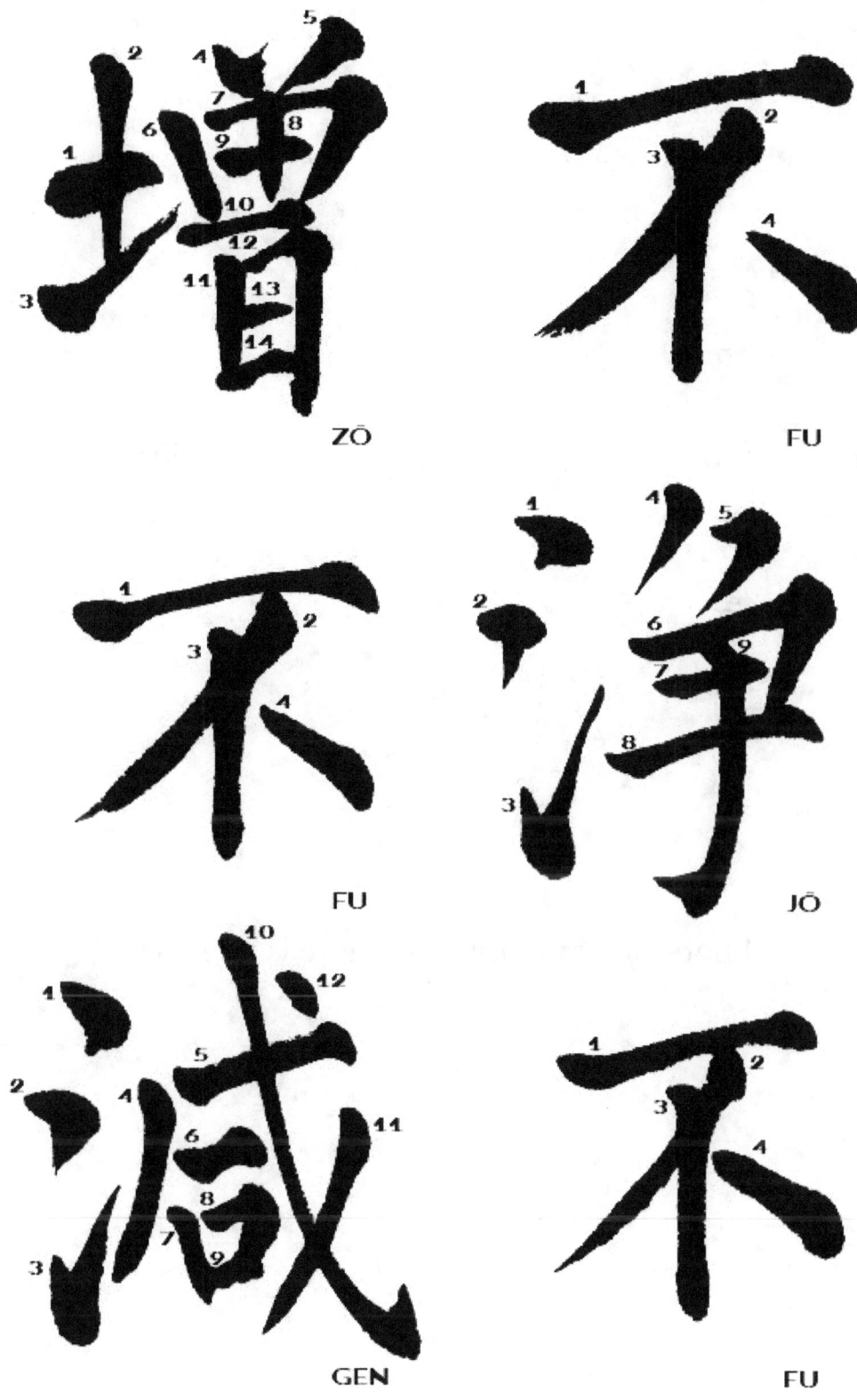

ZŌ

FU

FU

JŌ

GEN

FU

是	ZE	therefore
故	KO	
空	KŪ	emptiness
中	CHŪ	in
無	MU	no
色	SHIKI	form

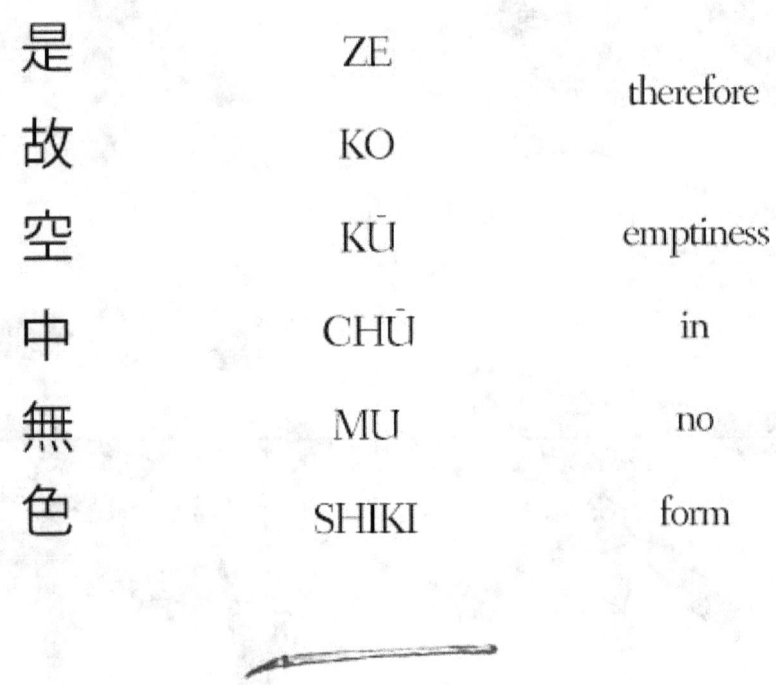

Therefore, in emptiness there is no form,

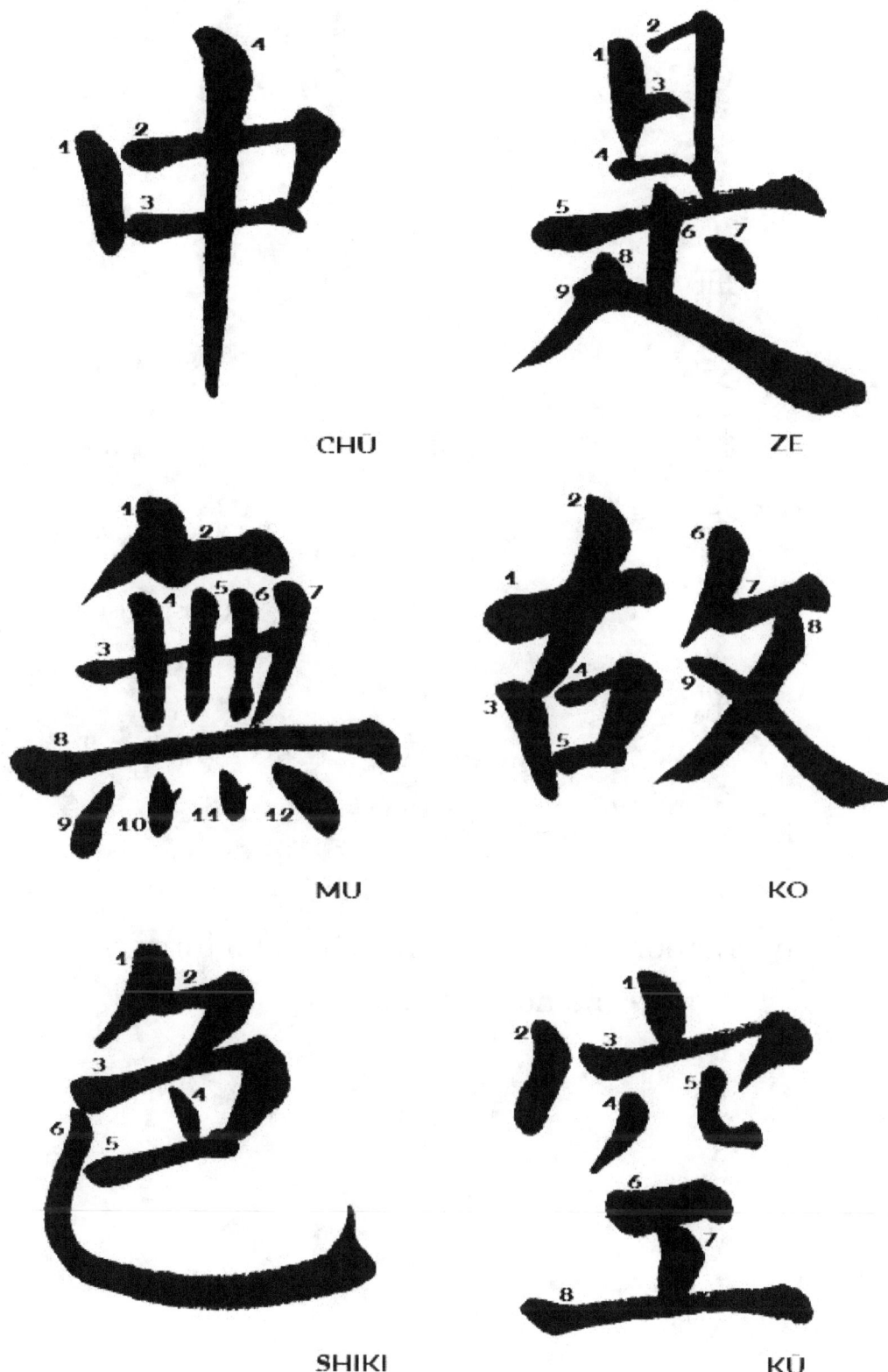

CHŪ   ZE

MU   KO

SHIKI   KŪ

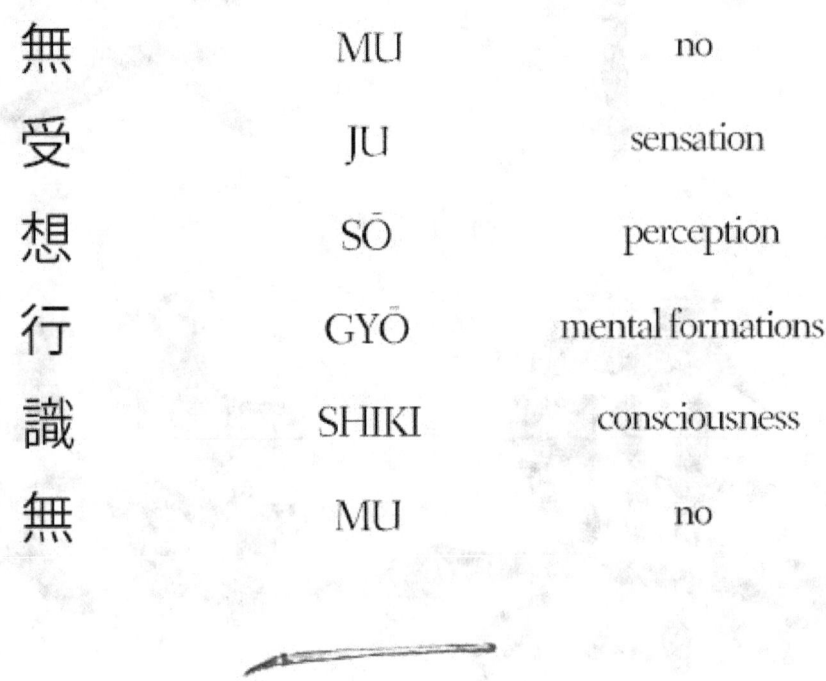

無	MU	no
受	JU	sensation
想	SŌ	perception
行	GYŌ	mental formations
識	SHIKI	consciousness
無	MU	no

no sensation, no perception, no mental formations
and no consciousness; no

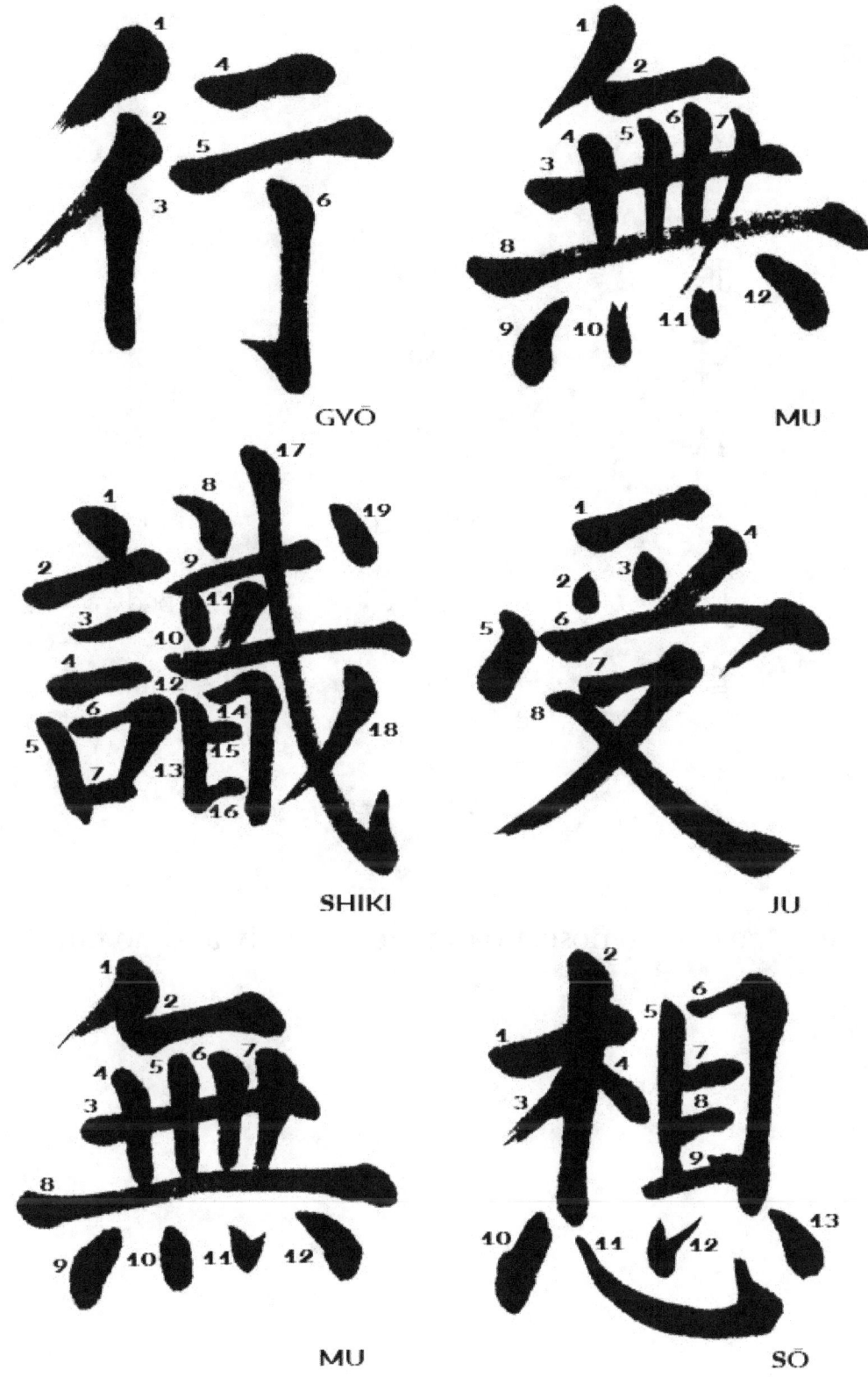

GYŌ

MU

SHIKI

JU

MU

SŌ

眼	GEN	eye
耳	NI	ear
鼻	BI	nose
舌	ZETSU	tongue
身	SHIN	body
意	I	mind

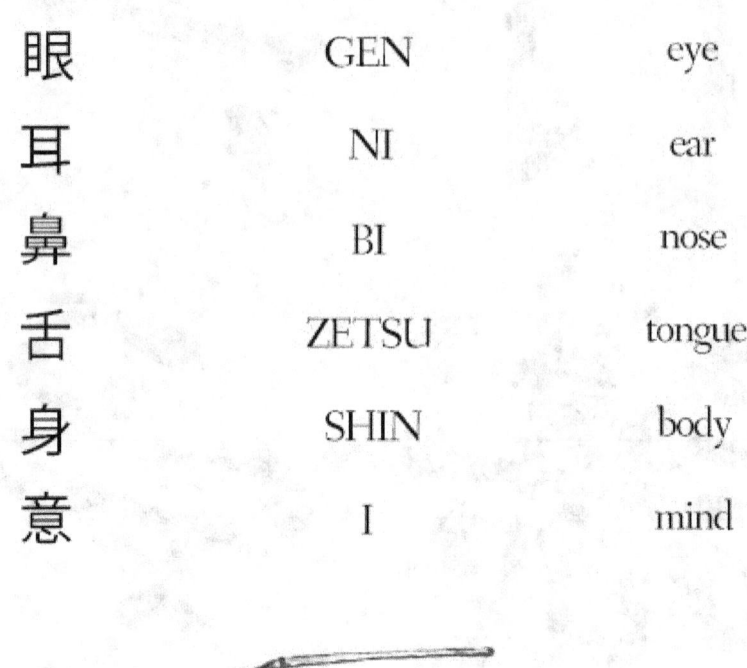

eye, no ear, no nose, no tongue, no body and no mind;

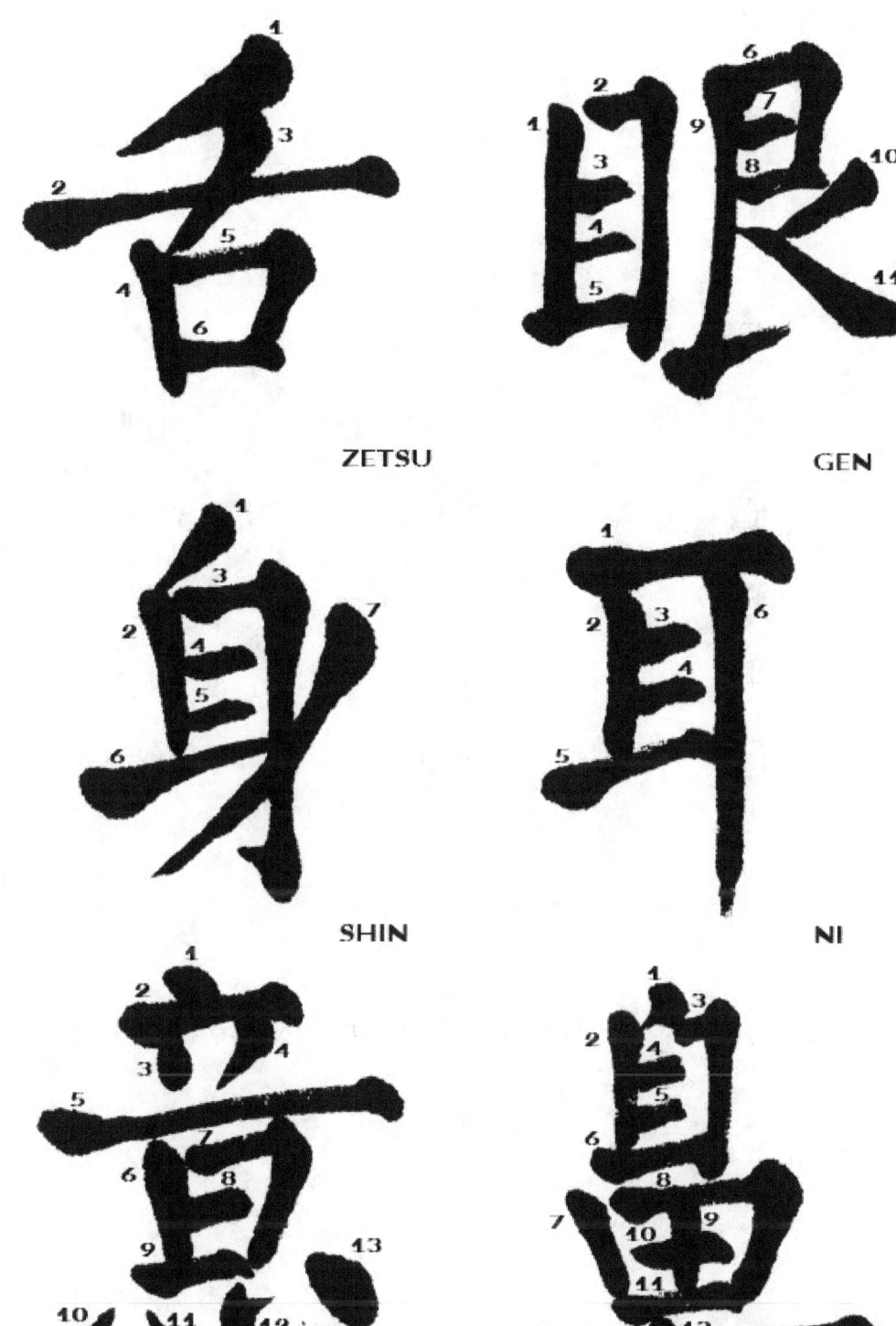

ZETSU

GEN

SHIN

NI

I

BI

無	MU	no
色	SHIKI	sight
聲	SHŌ	sound
香	KŌ	smell
味	MI	taste
觸	SOKU	feeeling

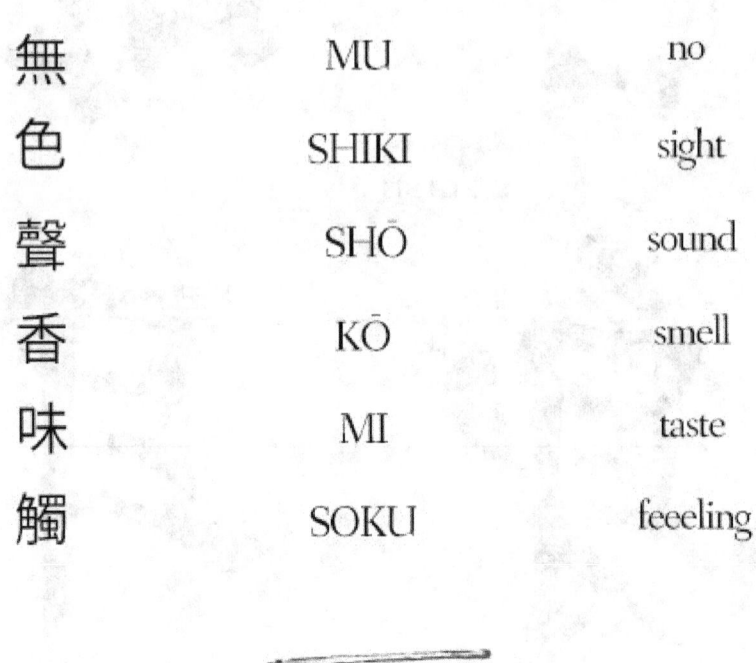

no sight, no sound, no smell, no taste, no feeling,

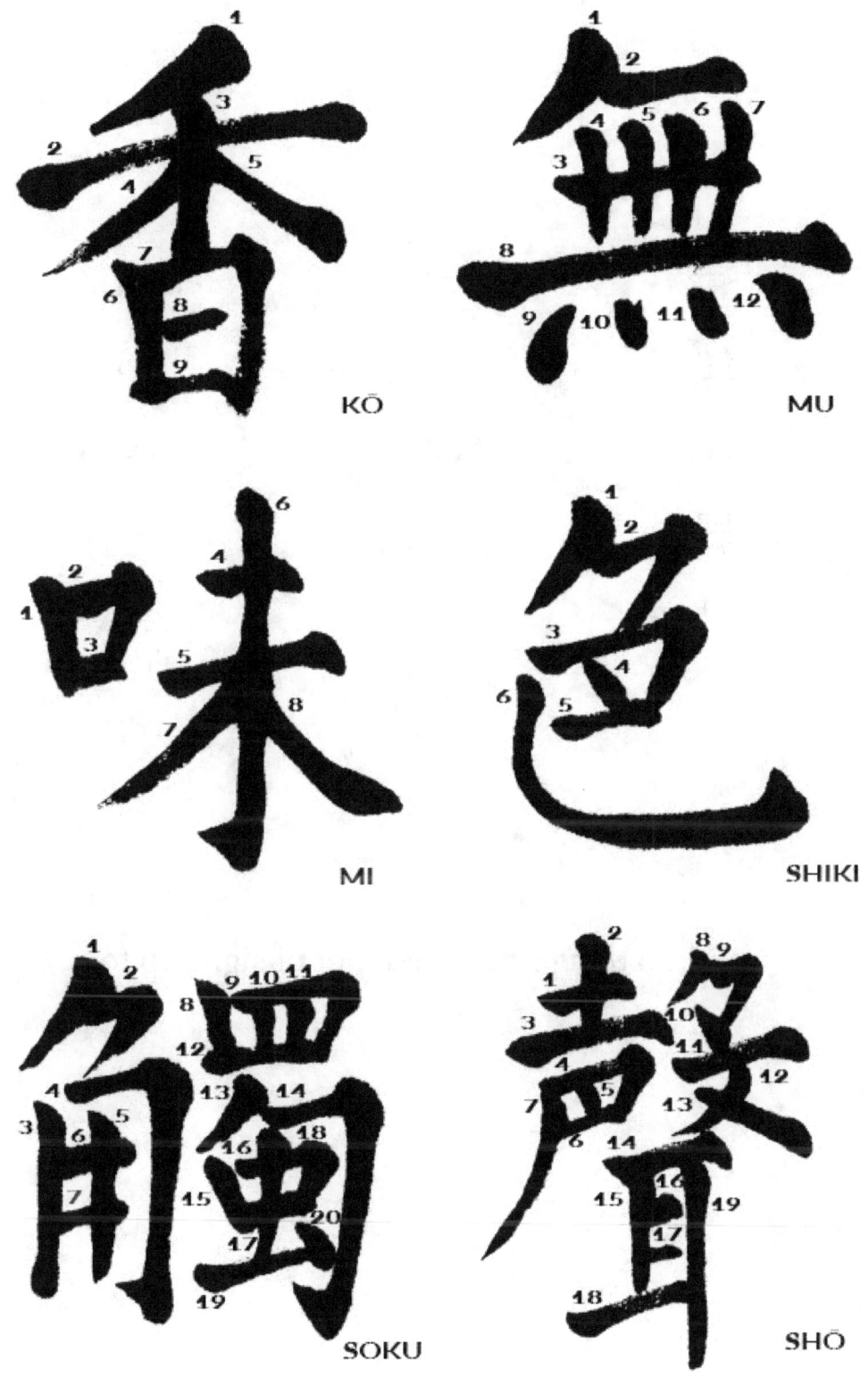

KŌ

MU

MI

SHIKI

SOKU

SHŌ

法	HŌ	thought
無	MU	no
眼	GEN	eye
界	KAI	element
乃	NAI	up to
至	SHI	

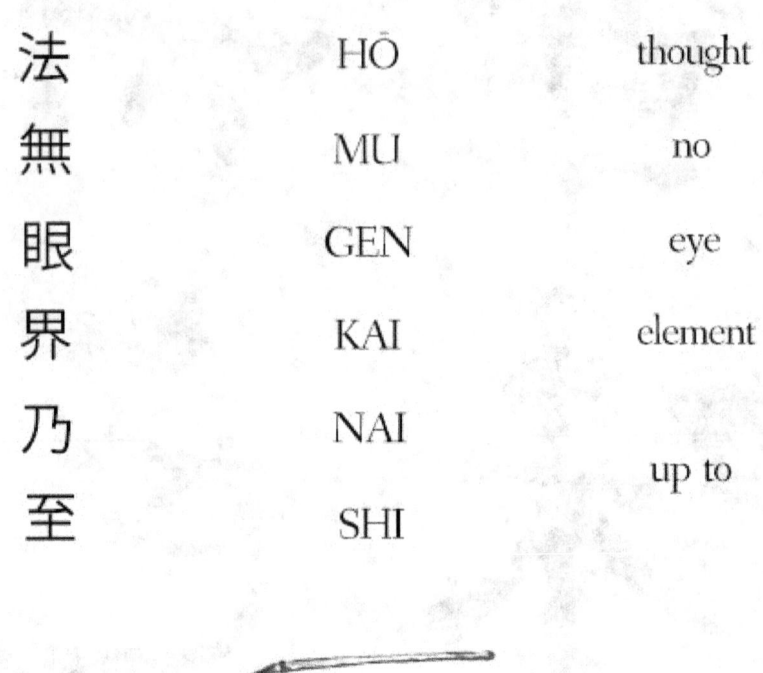

and no thought; no element of sight up to

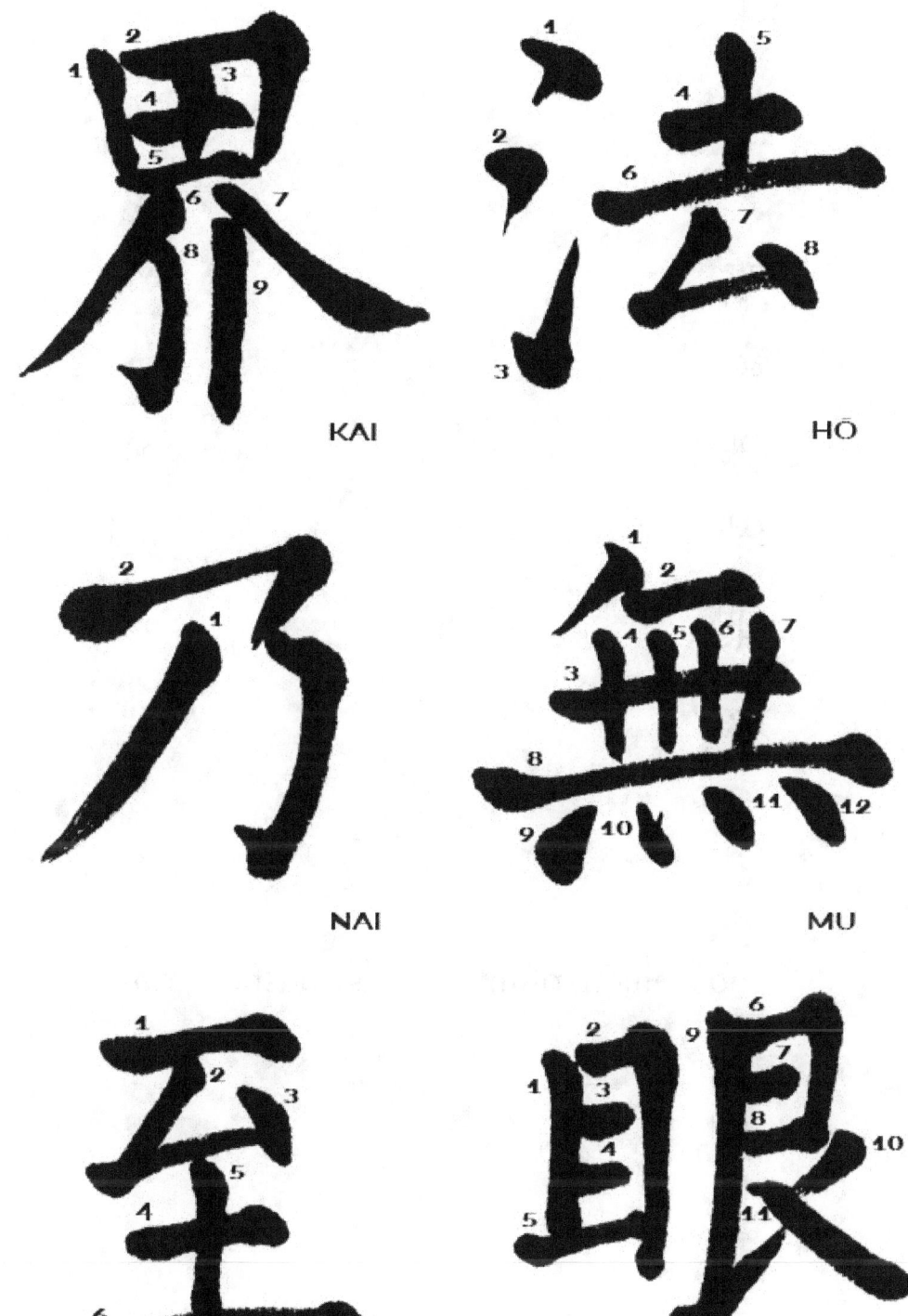

KAI

HŌ

NAI

MU

SHI

GEN

無	MU	no
意	I	mind
識	SHIKI	consciousness
界	KAI	element
無	MU	no
無	MU	ignorance

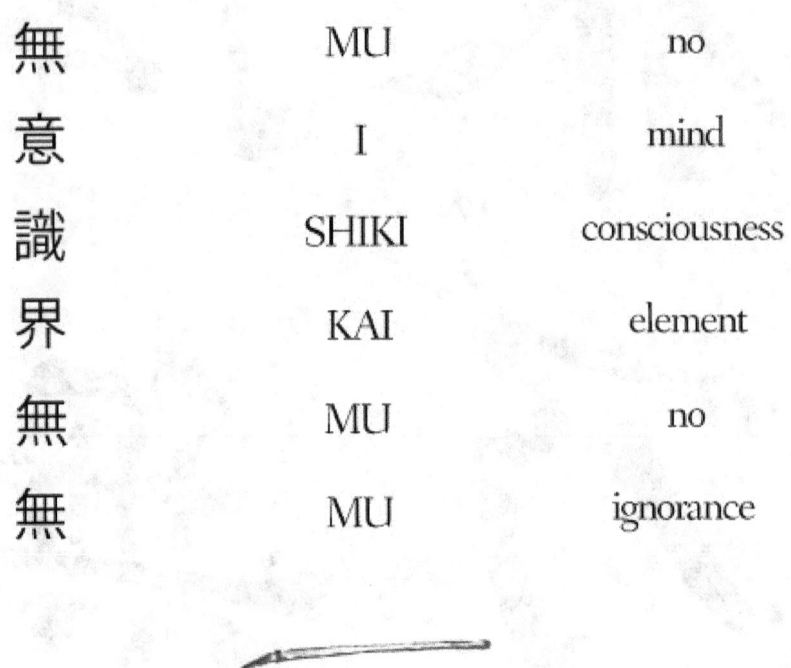

no element of mind-consciousness; no

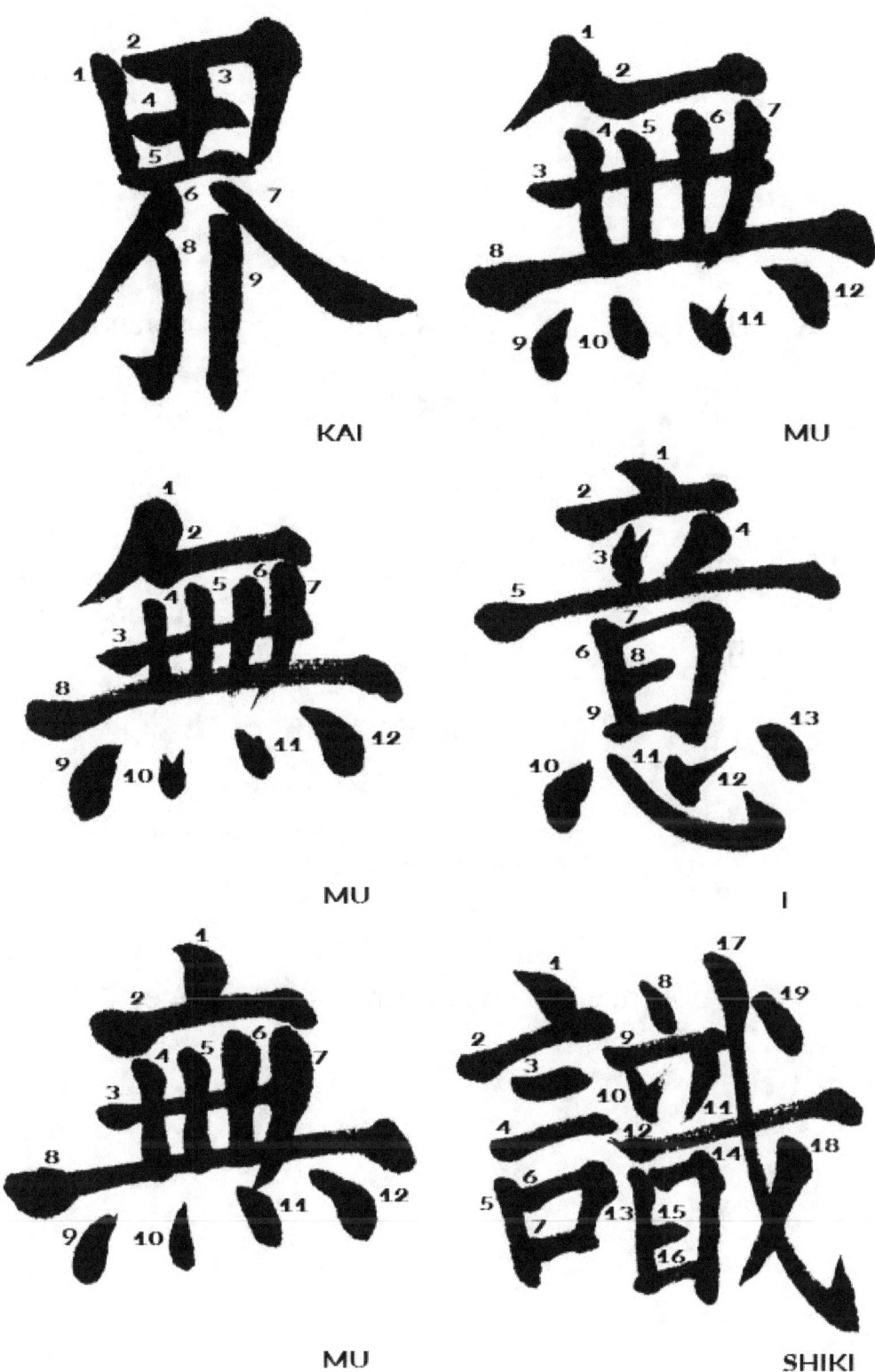

KAI

MU

MU

I

MU

SHIKI

明	MYŌ	ignorance
亦	YAKU	also
無	MU	no
無	MU	
明	MYŌ	ignorance
盡	JIN	end

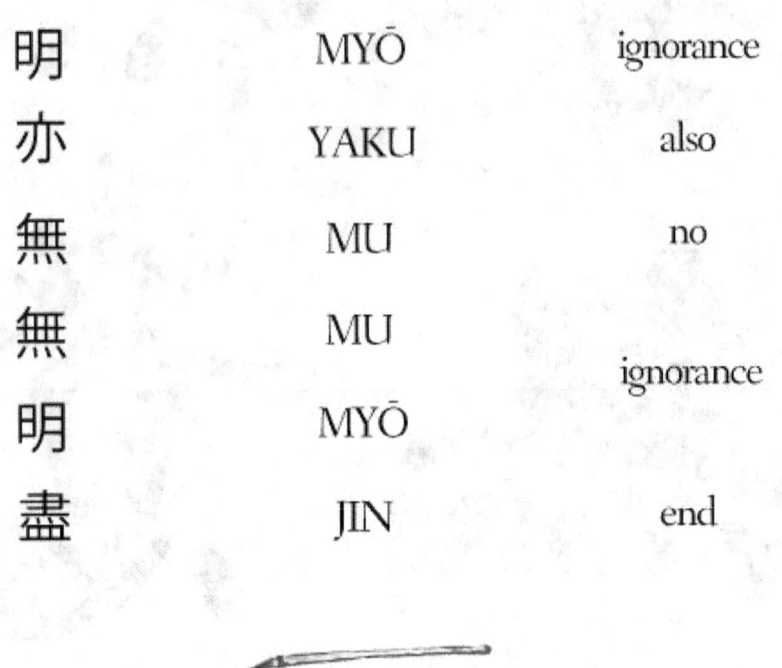

ignorance, and no ending of ignorance,

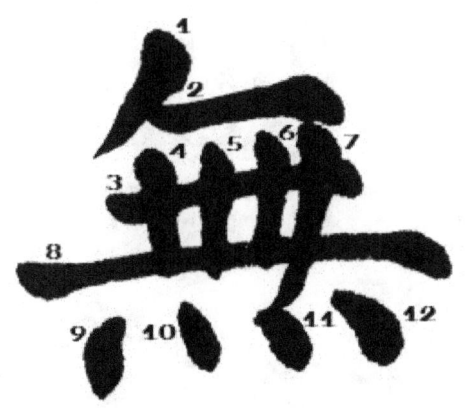

MU

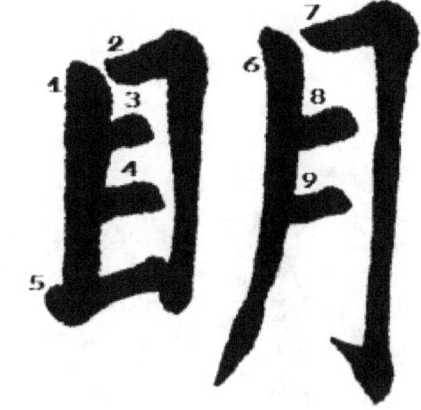

MYŌ

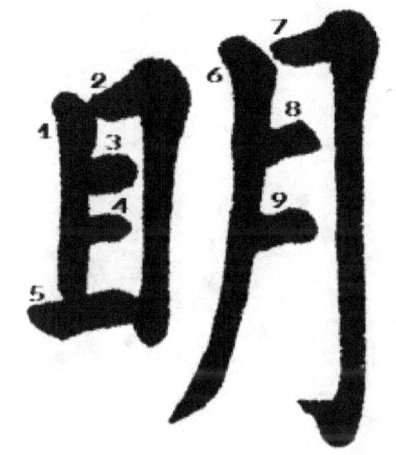

MYŌ

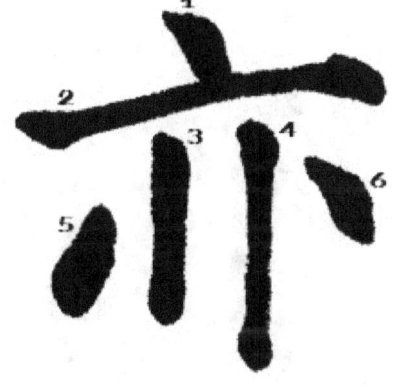

YAKU

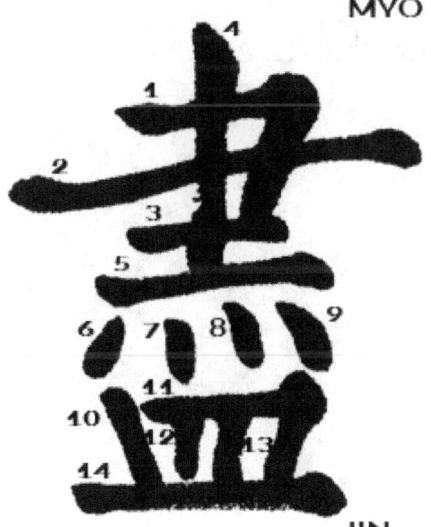

JIN

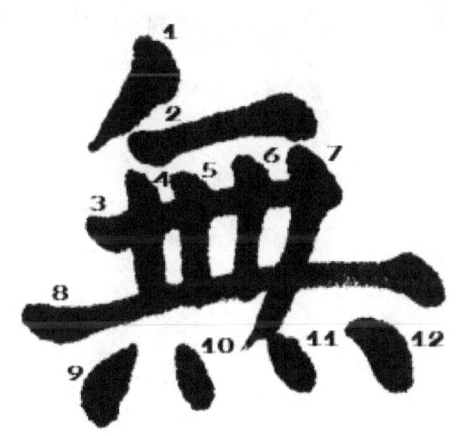

MU

乃	NAI	up to
至	SHI	
無	MU	no
老	RŌ	old age
死	SHI	death
亦	YAKU	also

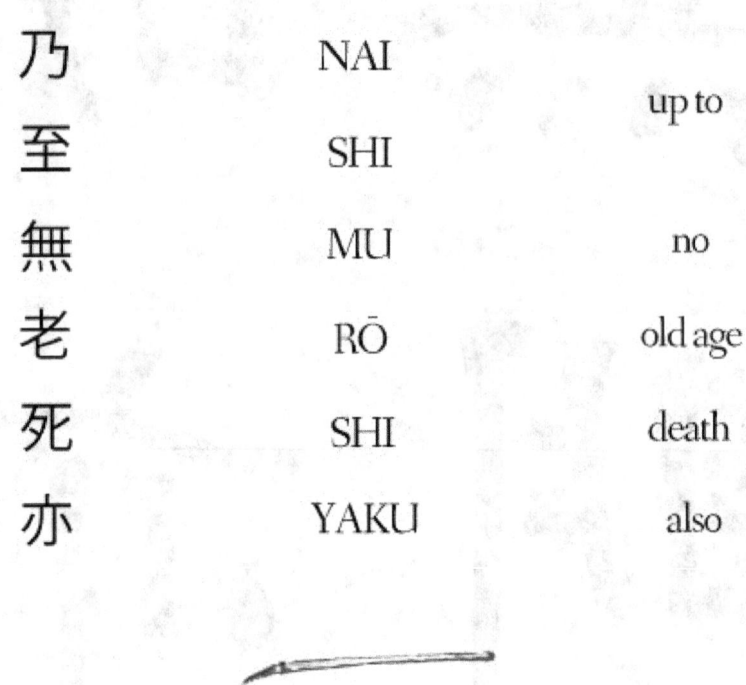

up to no old age and death, and

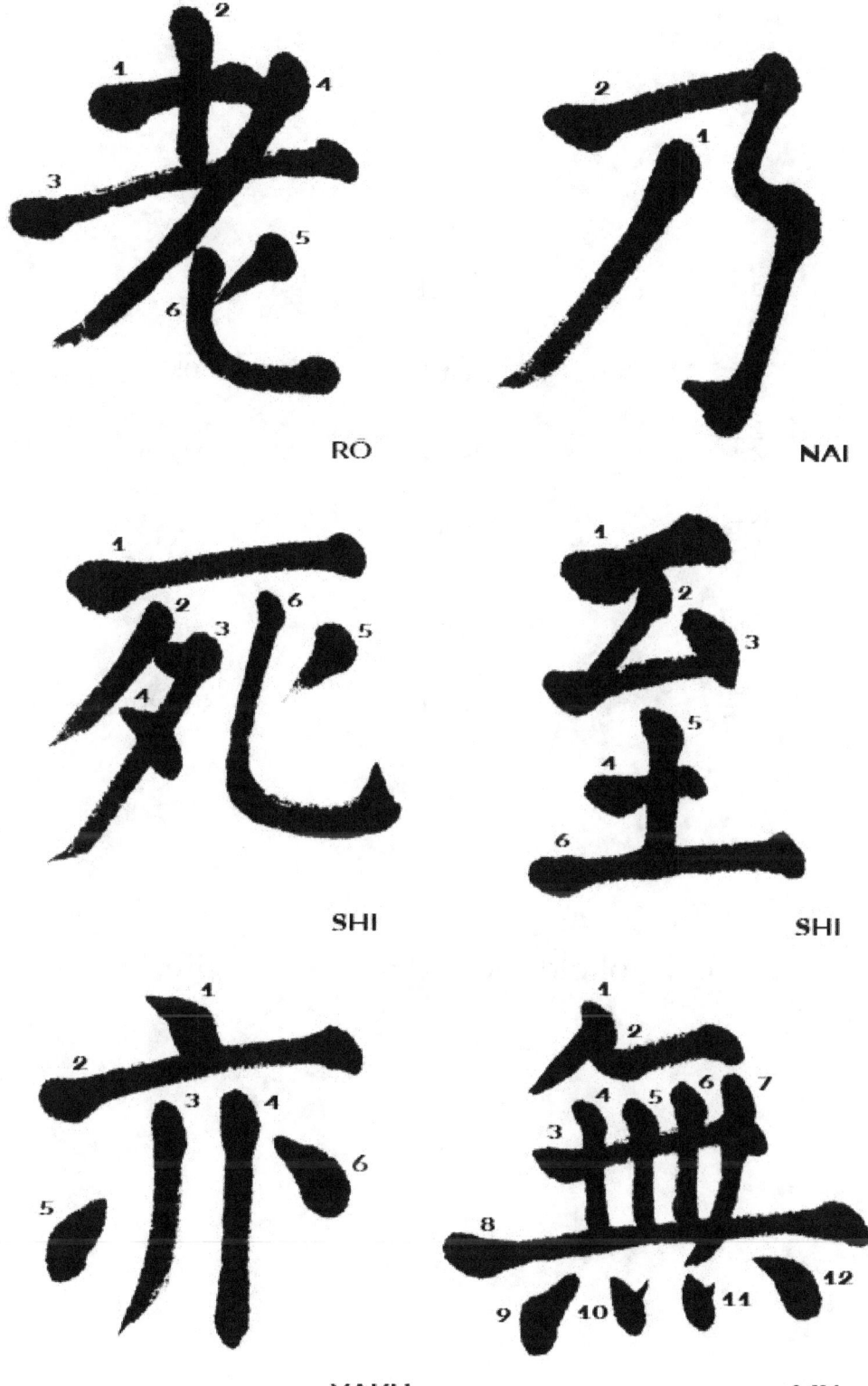

RŌ

NAI

SHI

SHI

YAKU

MU

無	MU	no
老	RŌ	old age
死	SHI	death
盡	JIN	end
無	MU	no
苦	KU	suffering

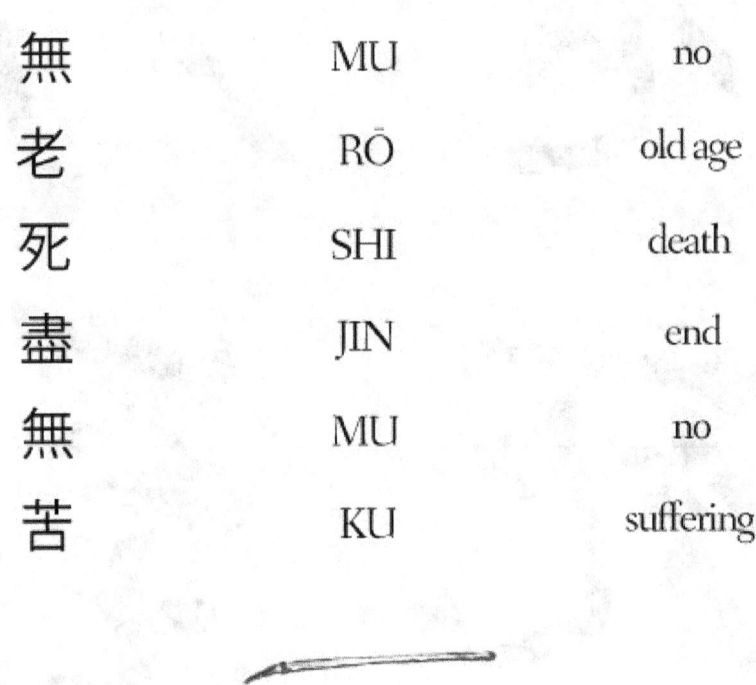

no ending of old age and death; no suffering,

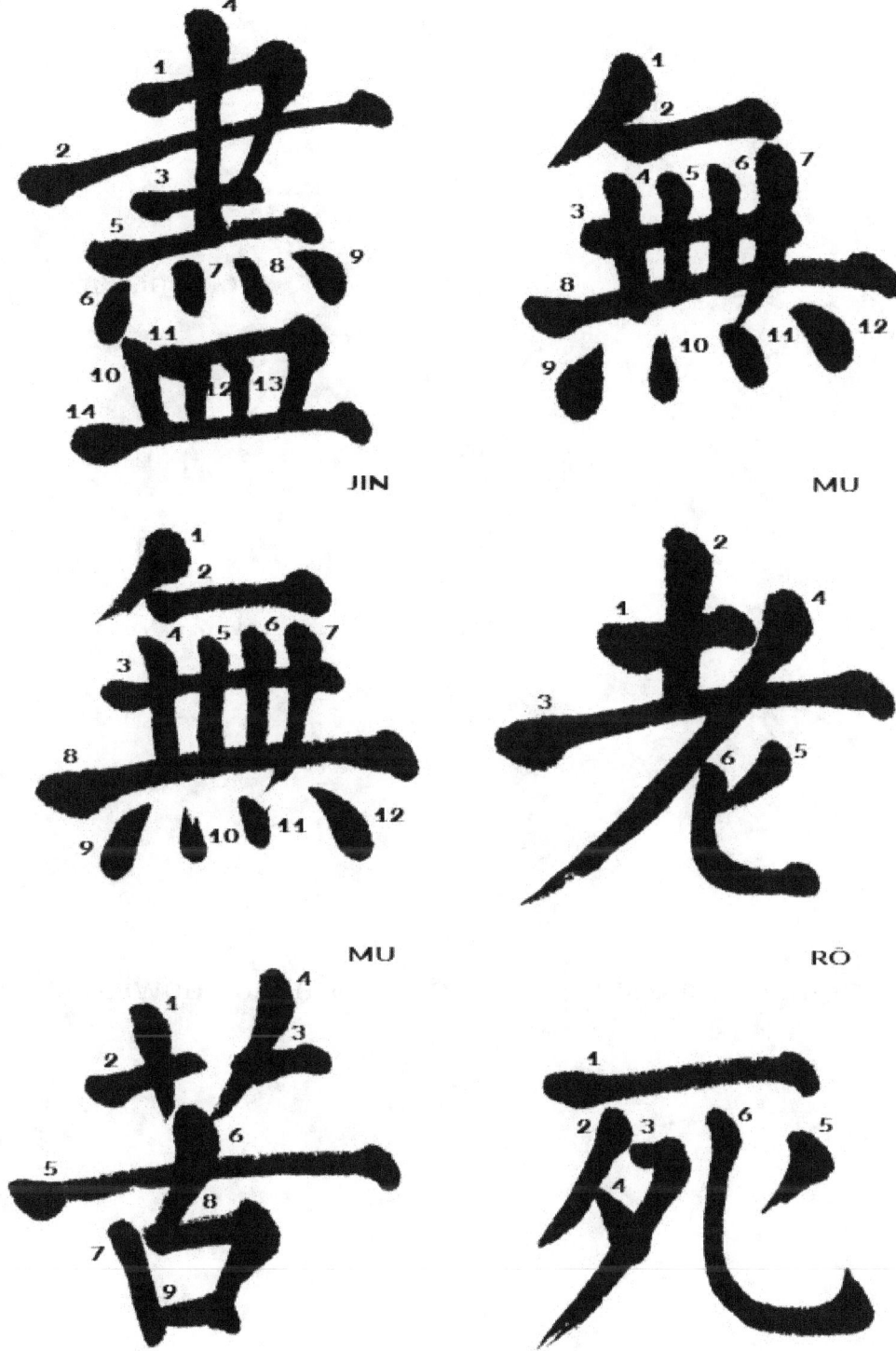

JIN

MU

MU

RŌ

KU

SHI

集	SHŪ	origination
滅	METSU	cessation
道	DŌ	path
無	MU	no
智	CHI	knowledge
亦	YAKU	also

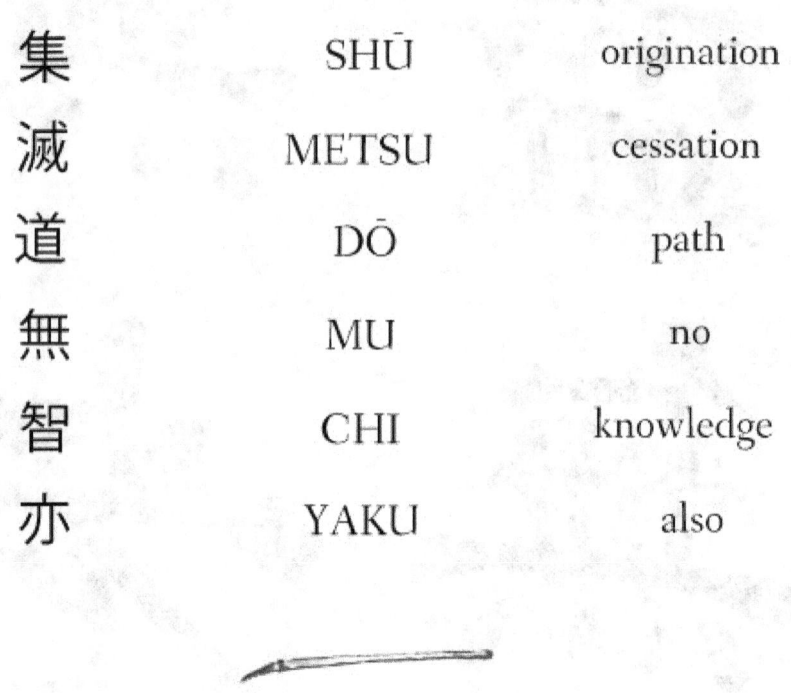

no origination, no stopping and no path; no knowledge and

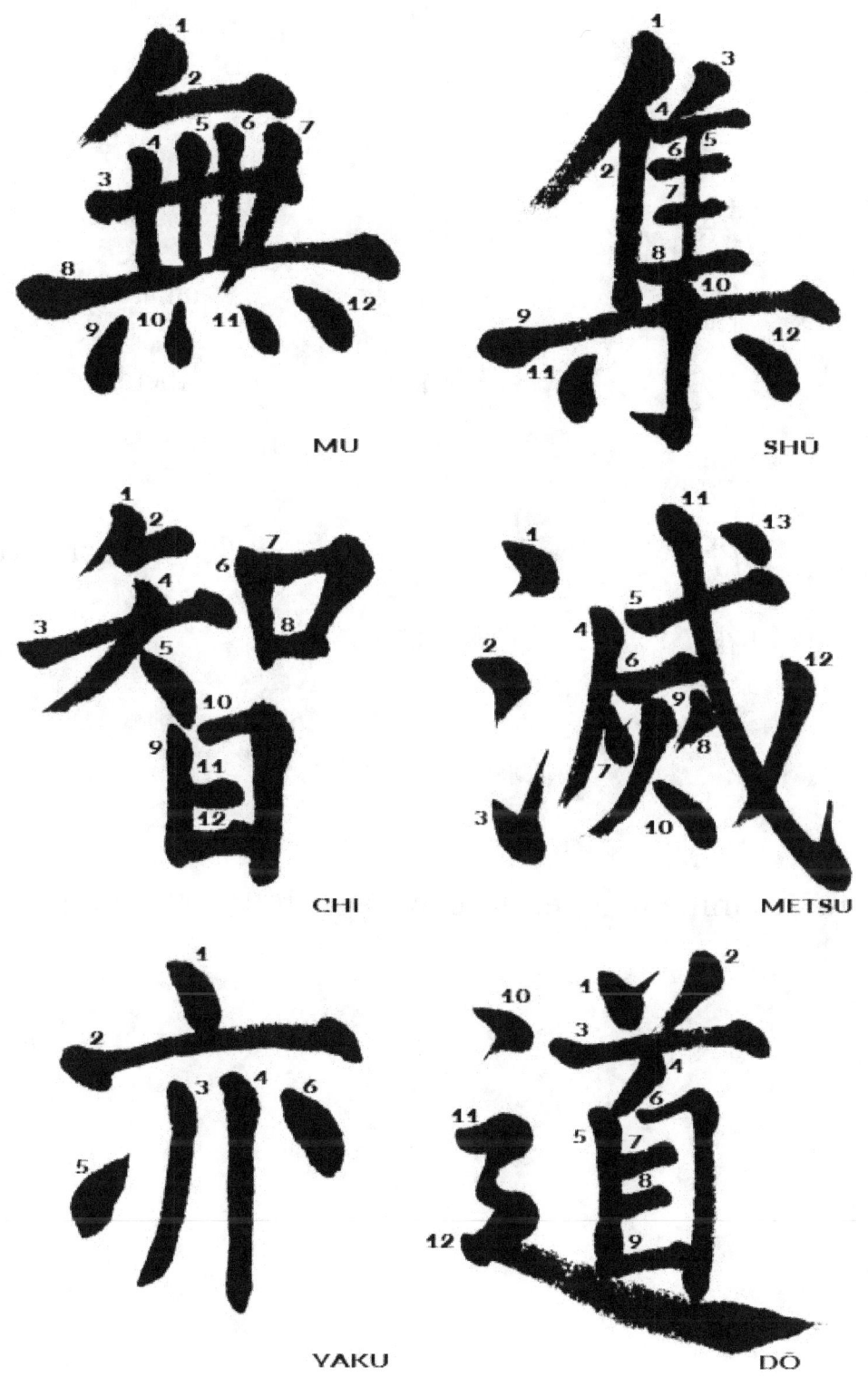

MU

SHŪ

CHI

METSU

YAKU

DŌ

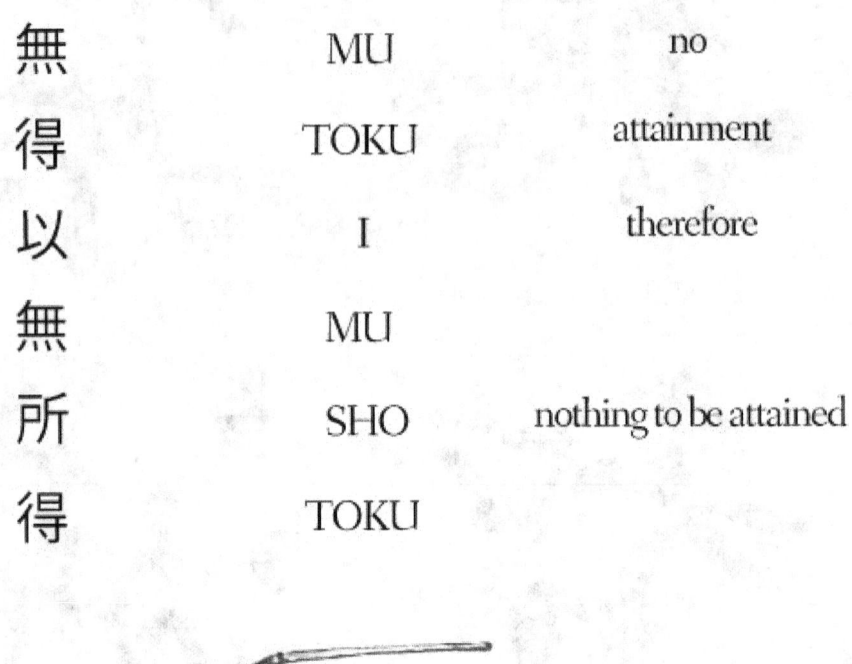

無	MU	no
得	TOKU	attainment
以	I	therefore
無	MU	
所	SHO	nothing to be attained
得	TOKU	

no attainment. Therefore, with nothing to be attained,

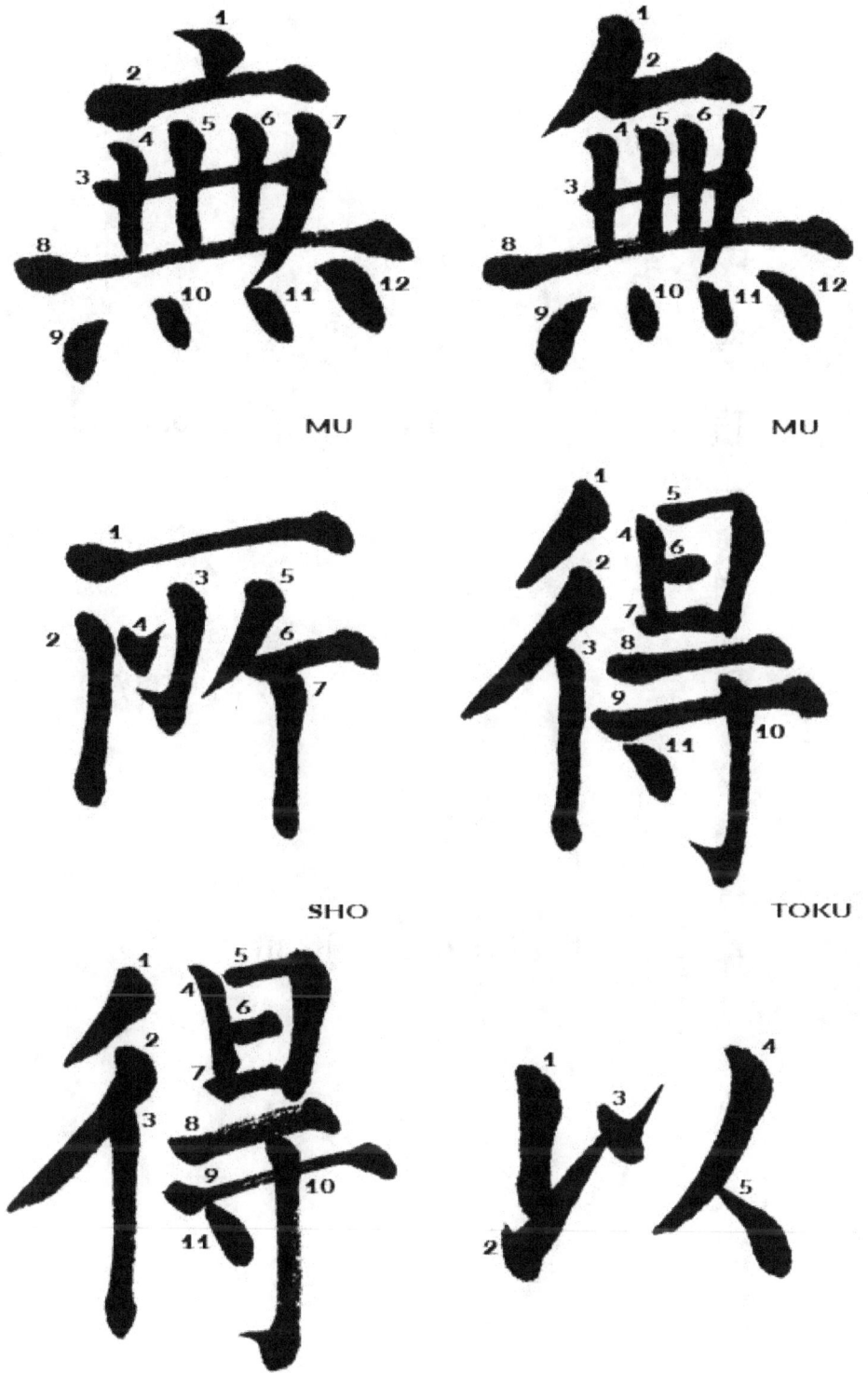

MU

MU

SHO

TOKU

TOKU

I

故　　KO　　　therefore

菩　　BO

提　　DAI　　　bodhisattva

薩　　SAT

埵　　TA

依　　E　　　　rely on

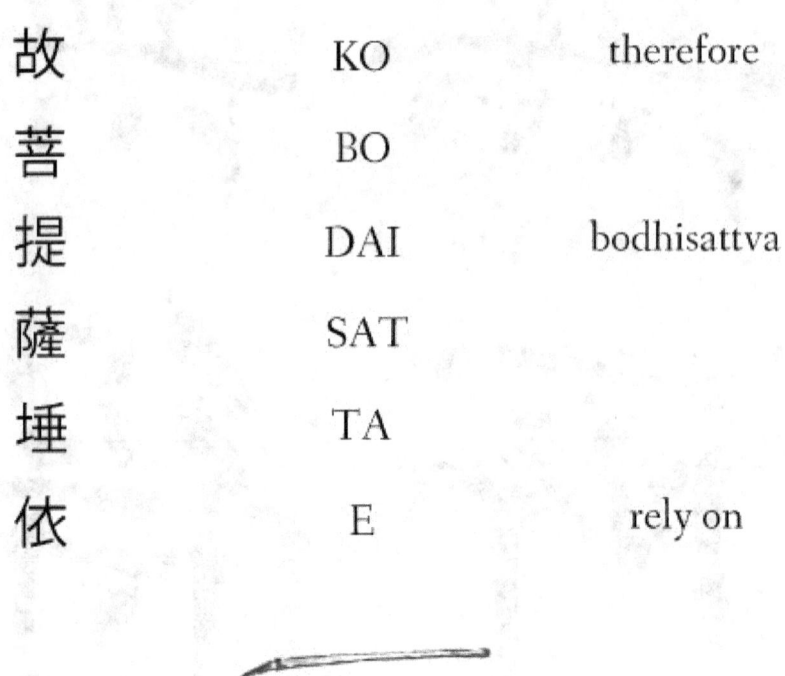

Bodhisattvas rely on

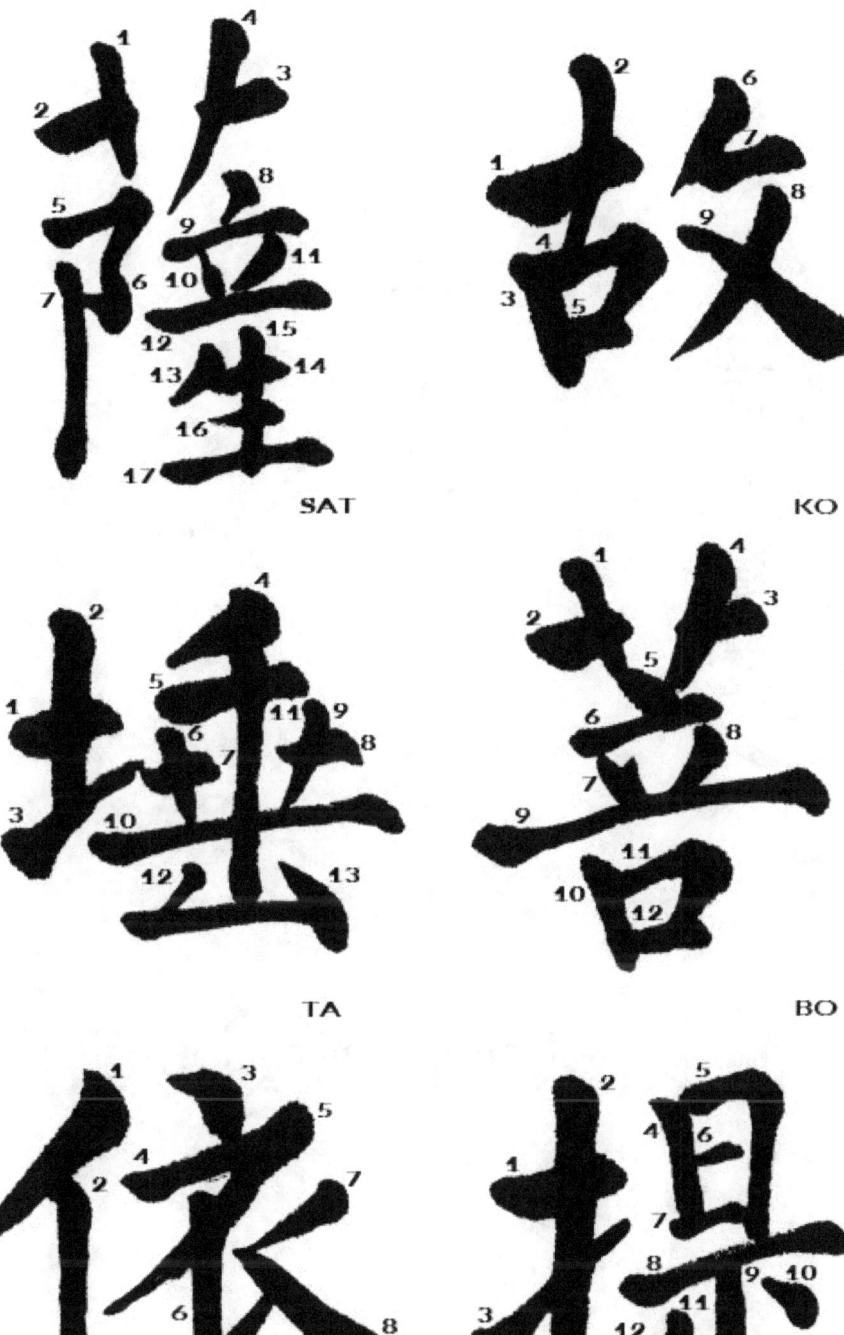

SAT

KO

TA

BO

E

DAI

般若波羅蜜多

HAN
NYA
HA
RA
MIT
TA

prajnaparamita

Prajnaparamita

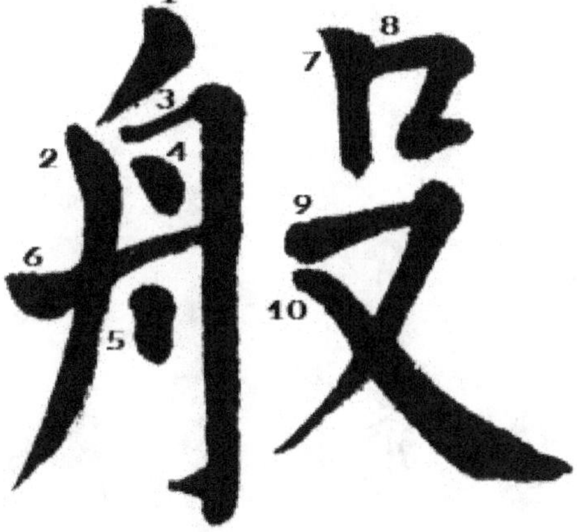

羅

般

RA   HAN

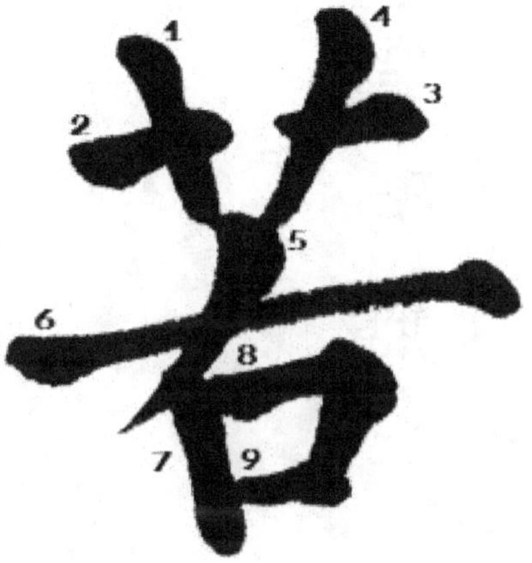

蜜

若

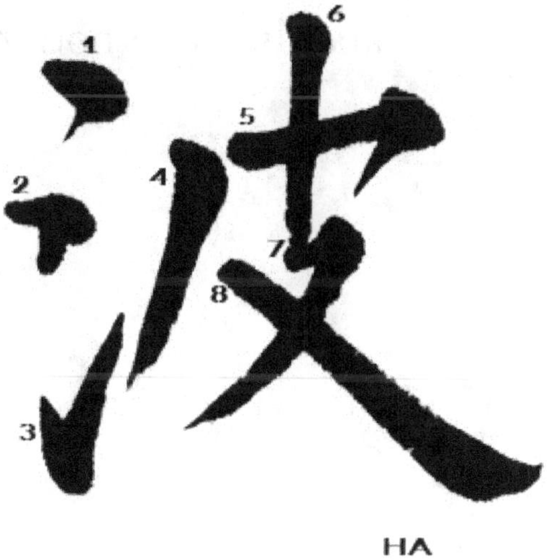

MIT   NYA

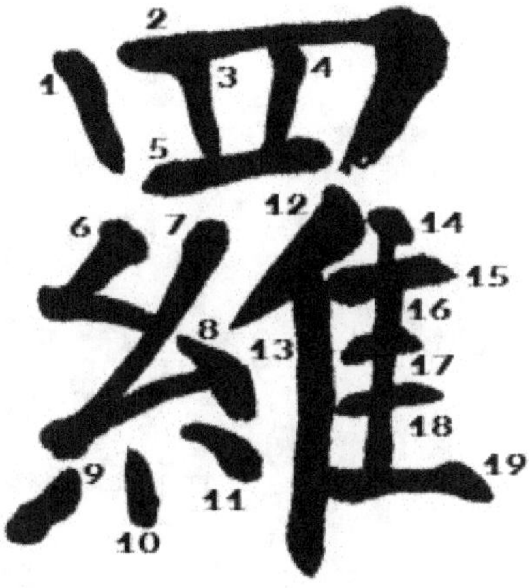

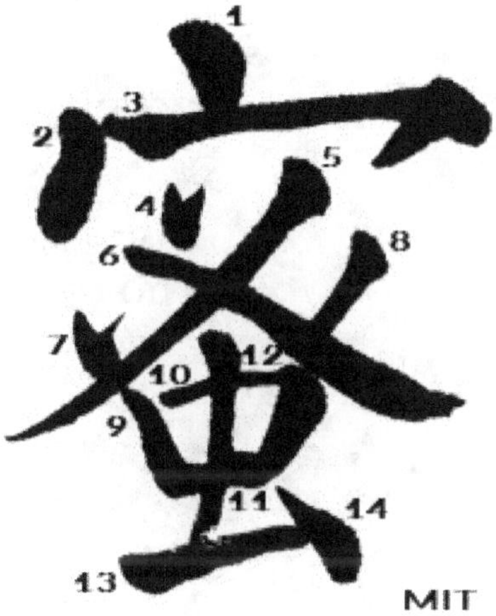

多

波

TA   HA

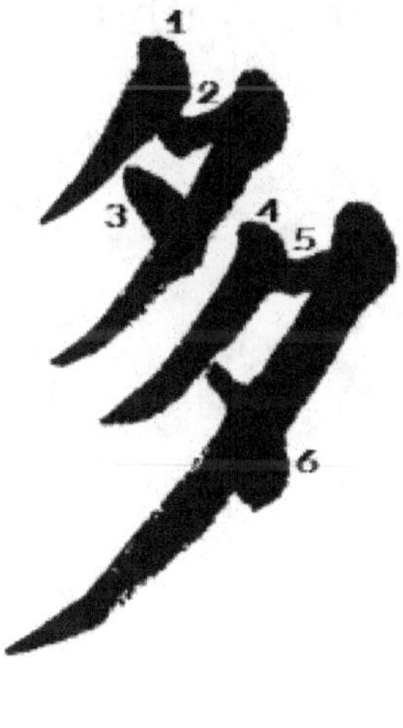

故	KO	therefore
心	SHIN	mind
無	MU	no
罣	KEI	
礙	GEI	barrier
無	MU	no

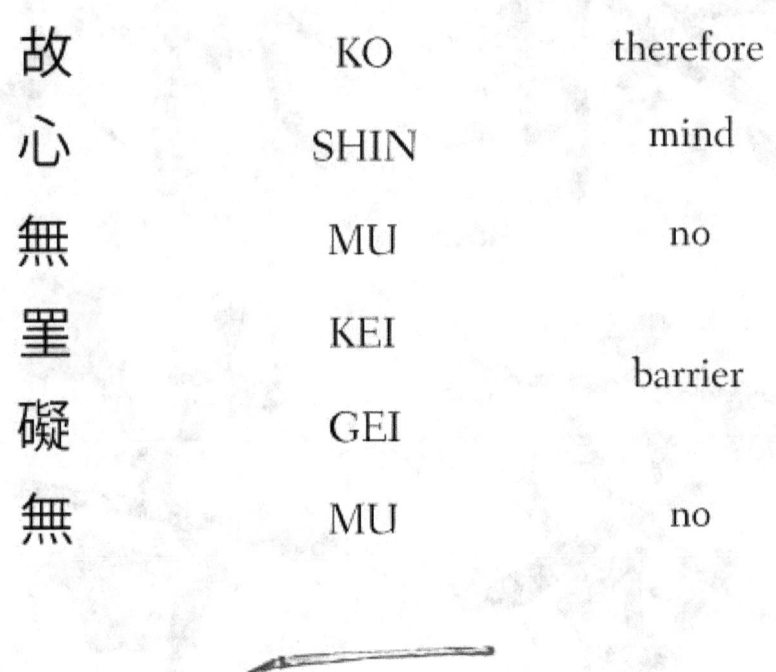

and dwell without mind barriers. Without

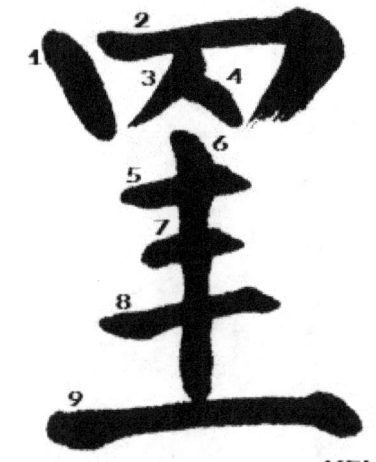

KEI

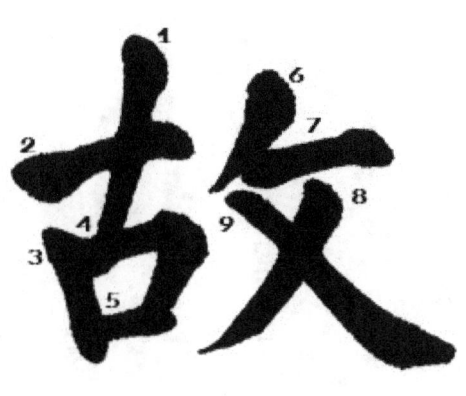

KO

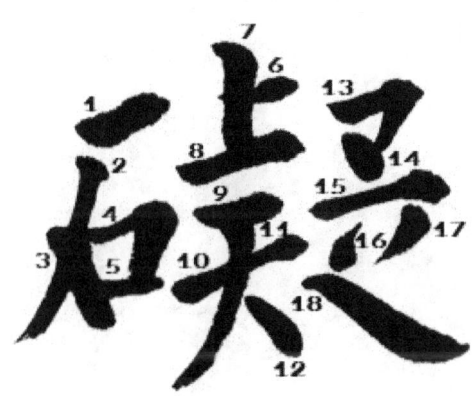

GEI

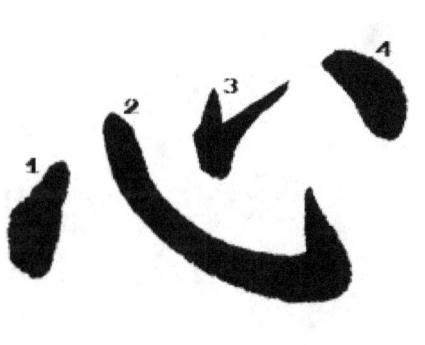

SHIN

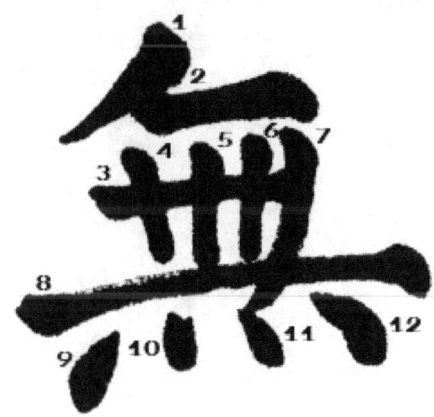

MU

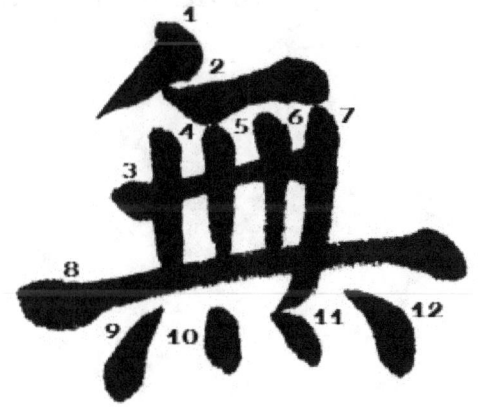

MU

罣	KEI	barrier
礙	GEI	
故	KO	therefore
無	MU	not
有	U	have
恐	KU(FU)	fear

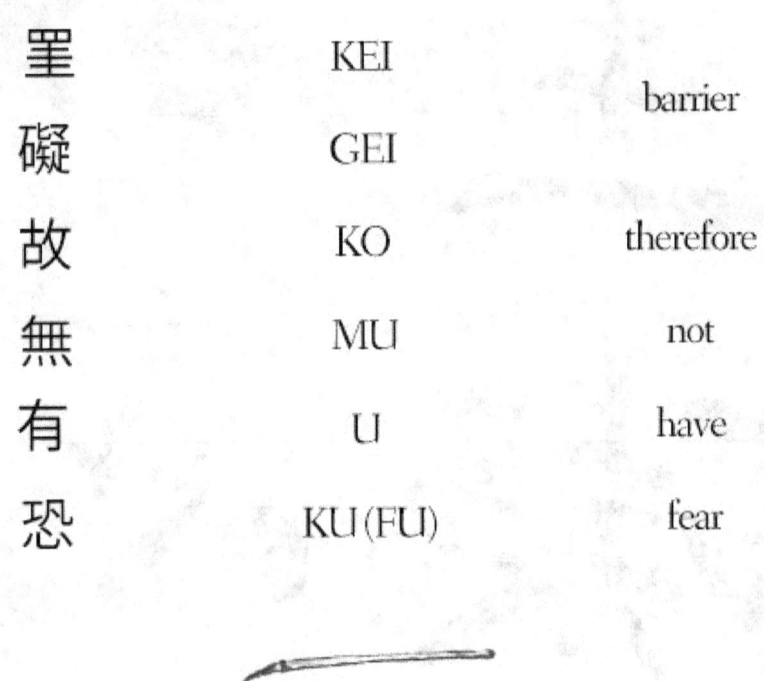

mind barriers and thus fearless,

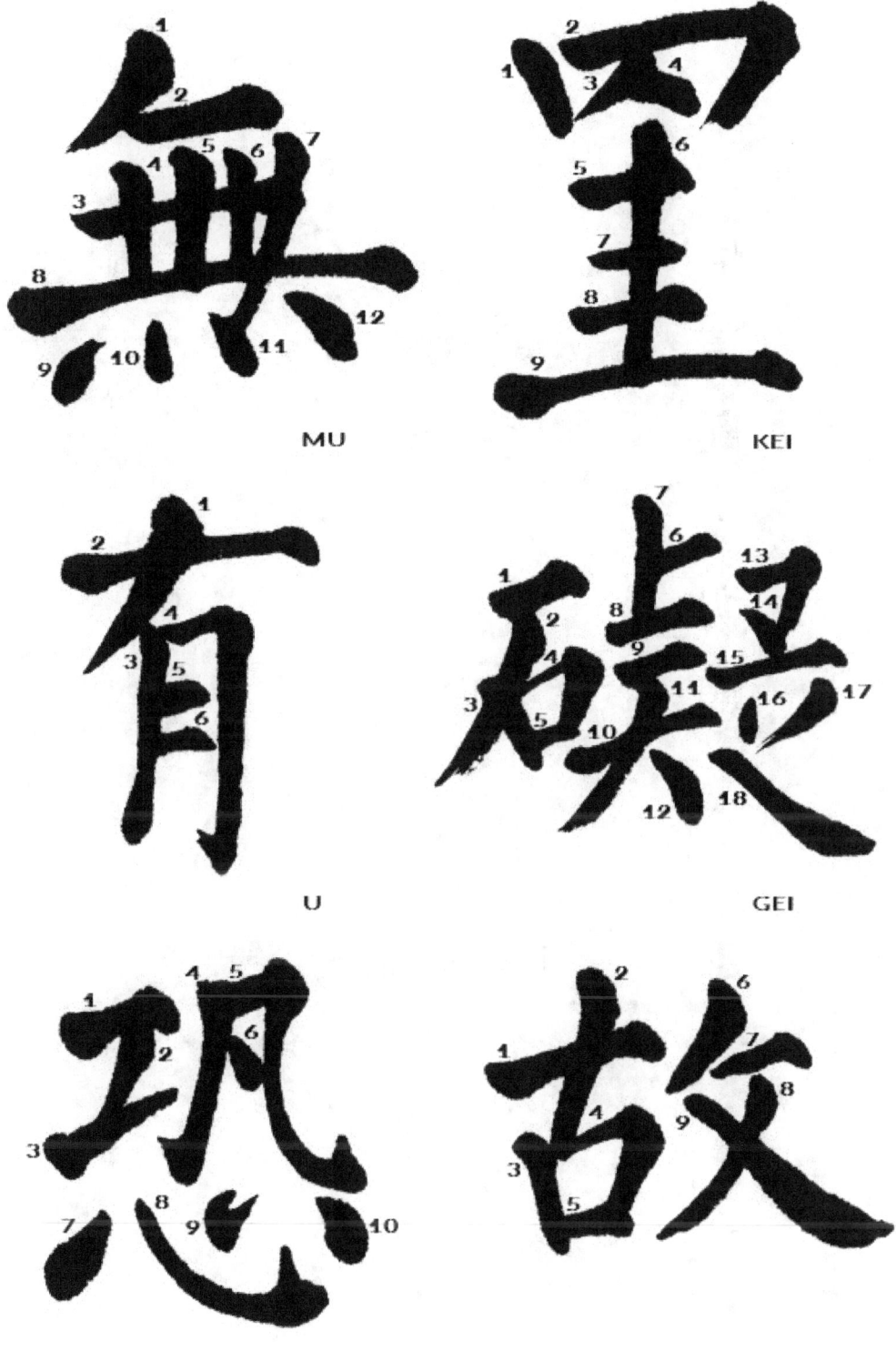

MU

KEI

U

GEI

KU

KO

怖　FU　fear

遠　ON

離　RI　transcend

一　IS

切　SAI　all

顚　TEN(DŌ)　distortion

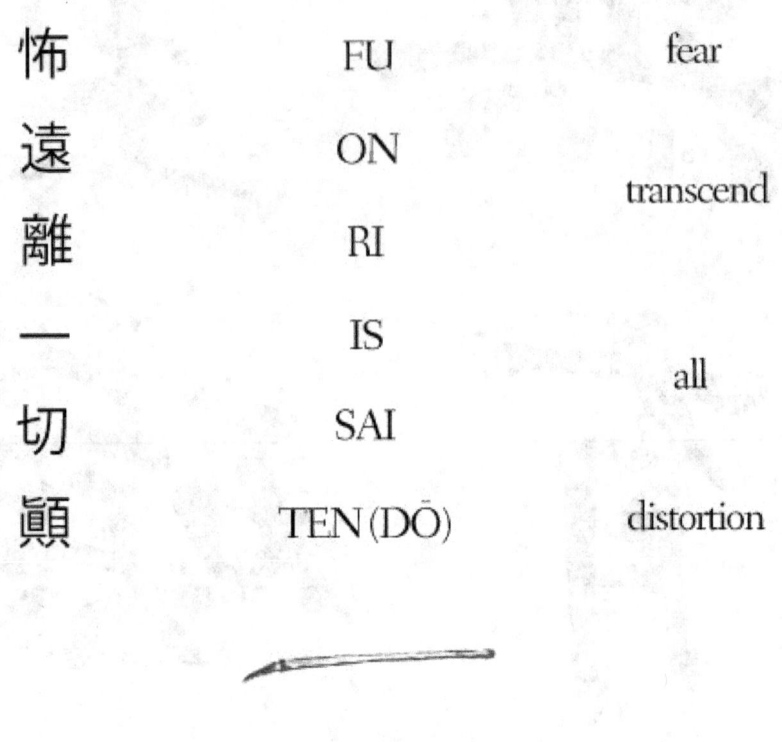

they see through

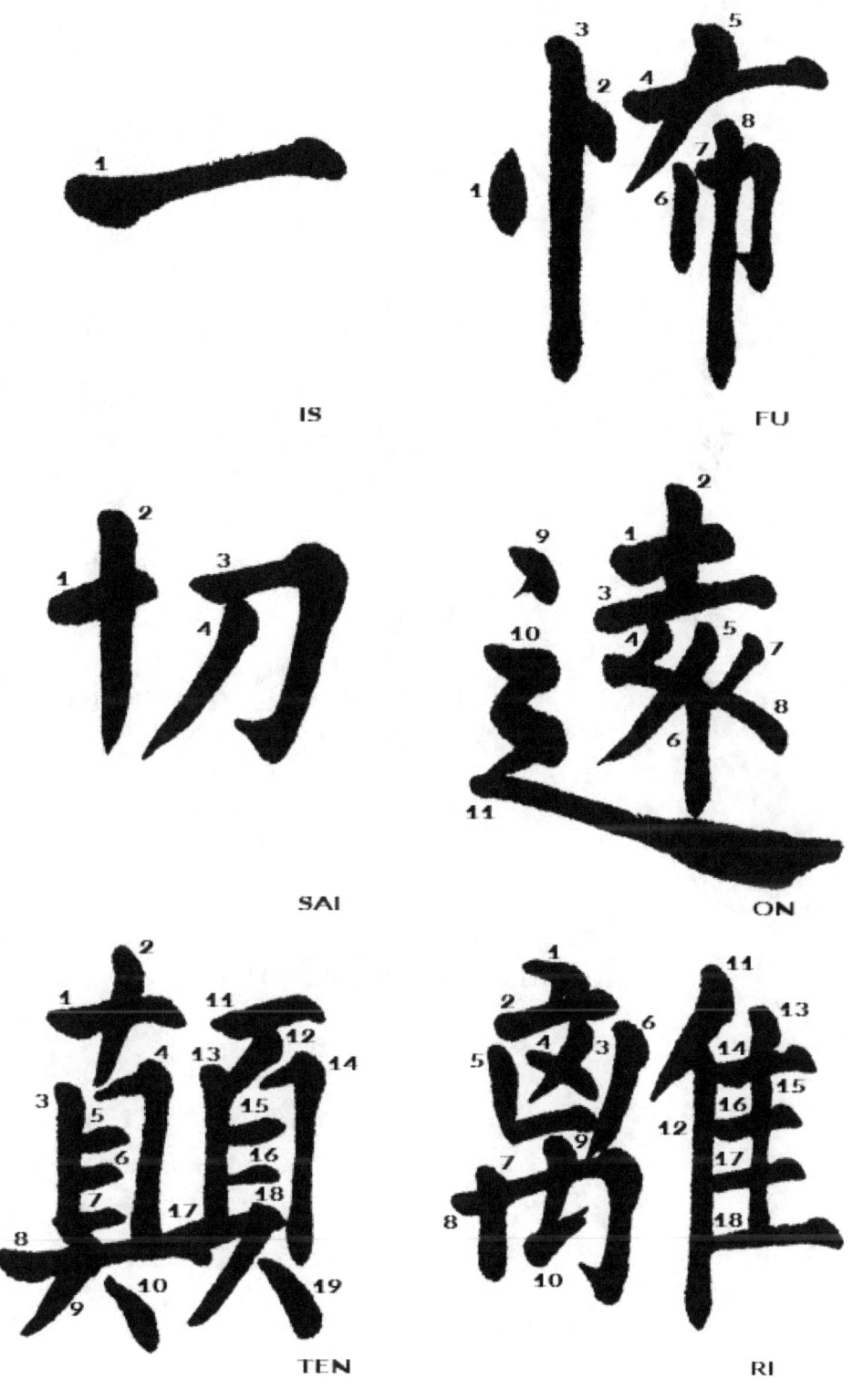

IS   FU

SAI   ON

TEN   RI

倒	DŌ	distortion
夢	MU	
想	SŌ	delusion
究	KU	
竟	GYŌ	finally
涅	NE(HAN)	nirvana

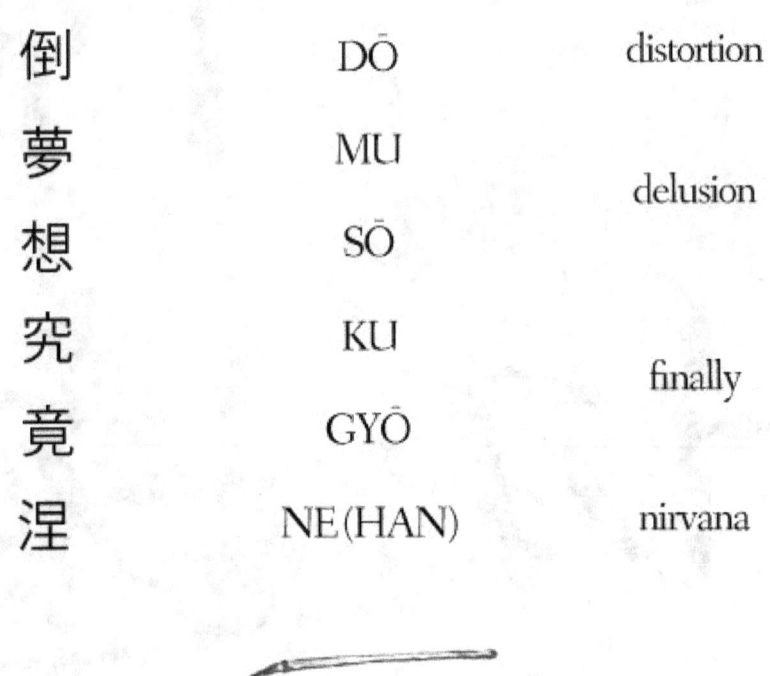

delusions and finally Nirvana.

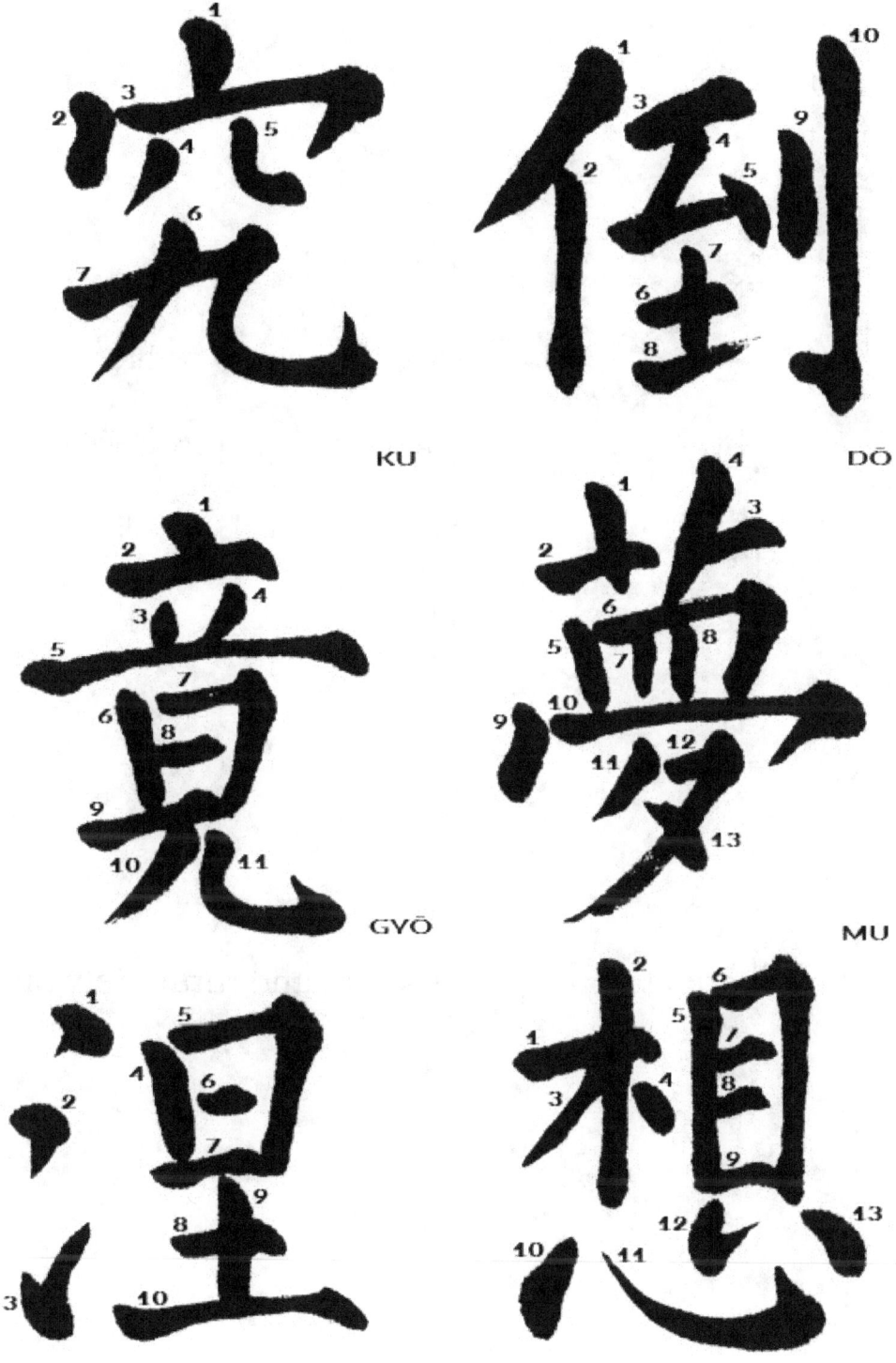

究 KU

倒 DŌ

竟 GYŌ

夢 MU

涅 NE

想 SŌ

槃	HAN	nirvana
三	SAN	three
世	ZE	period of time
諸	SHO	all
佛	BUTSU	buddha
依	E	rely on

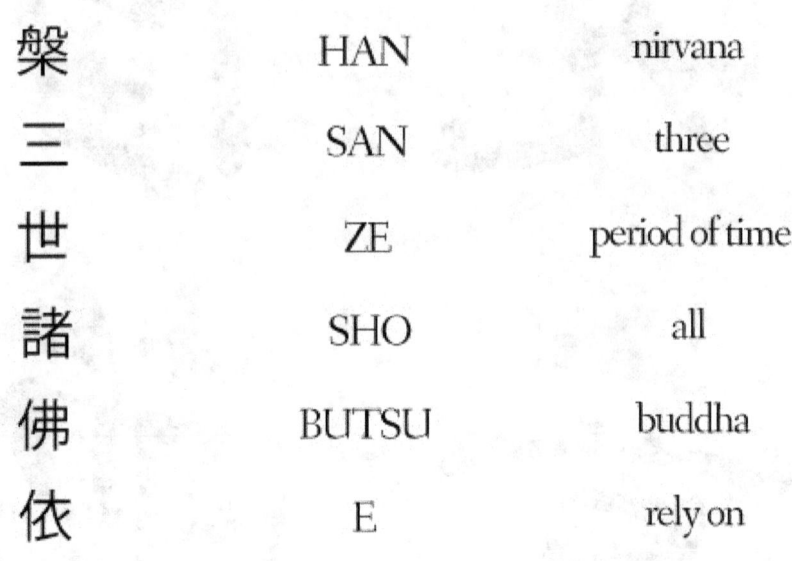

All Buddhas of the past, present and future rely on

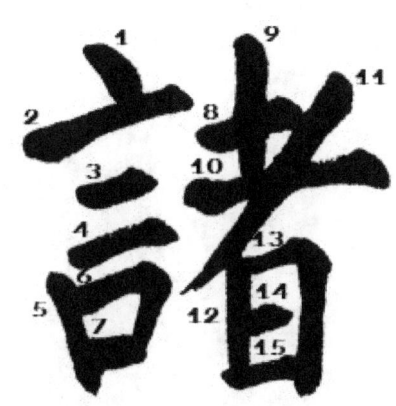
SHO

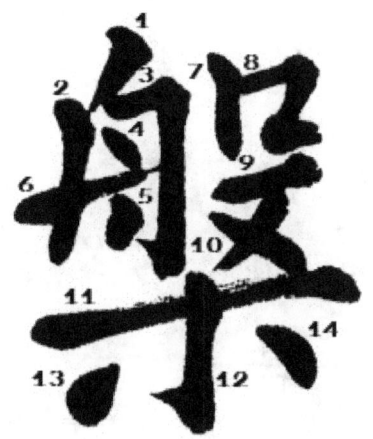

HAN

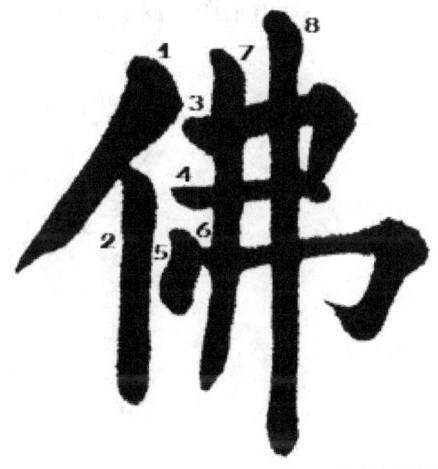
BUTSU

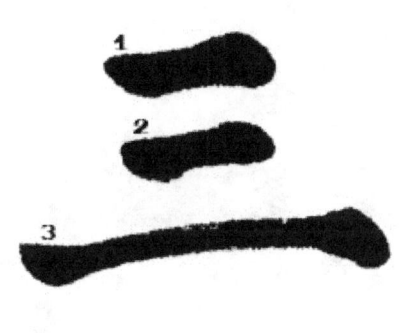
SAN

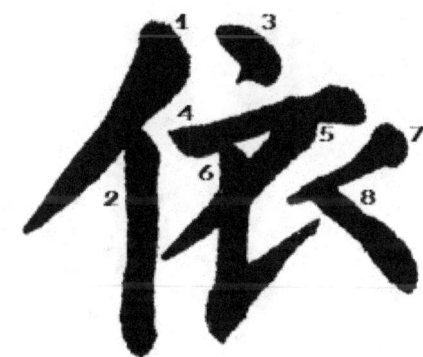
E

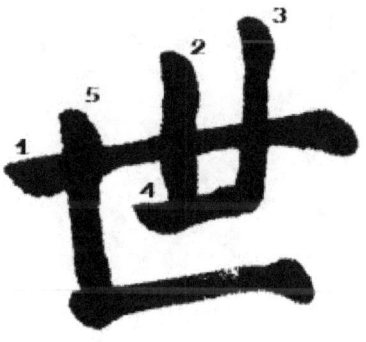
ZE

般　　HAN
若　　NYA
波　　HA
羅　　RA　　　　　prajnaparamita
蜜　　MIT
多　　TA

Prajnaparamita

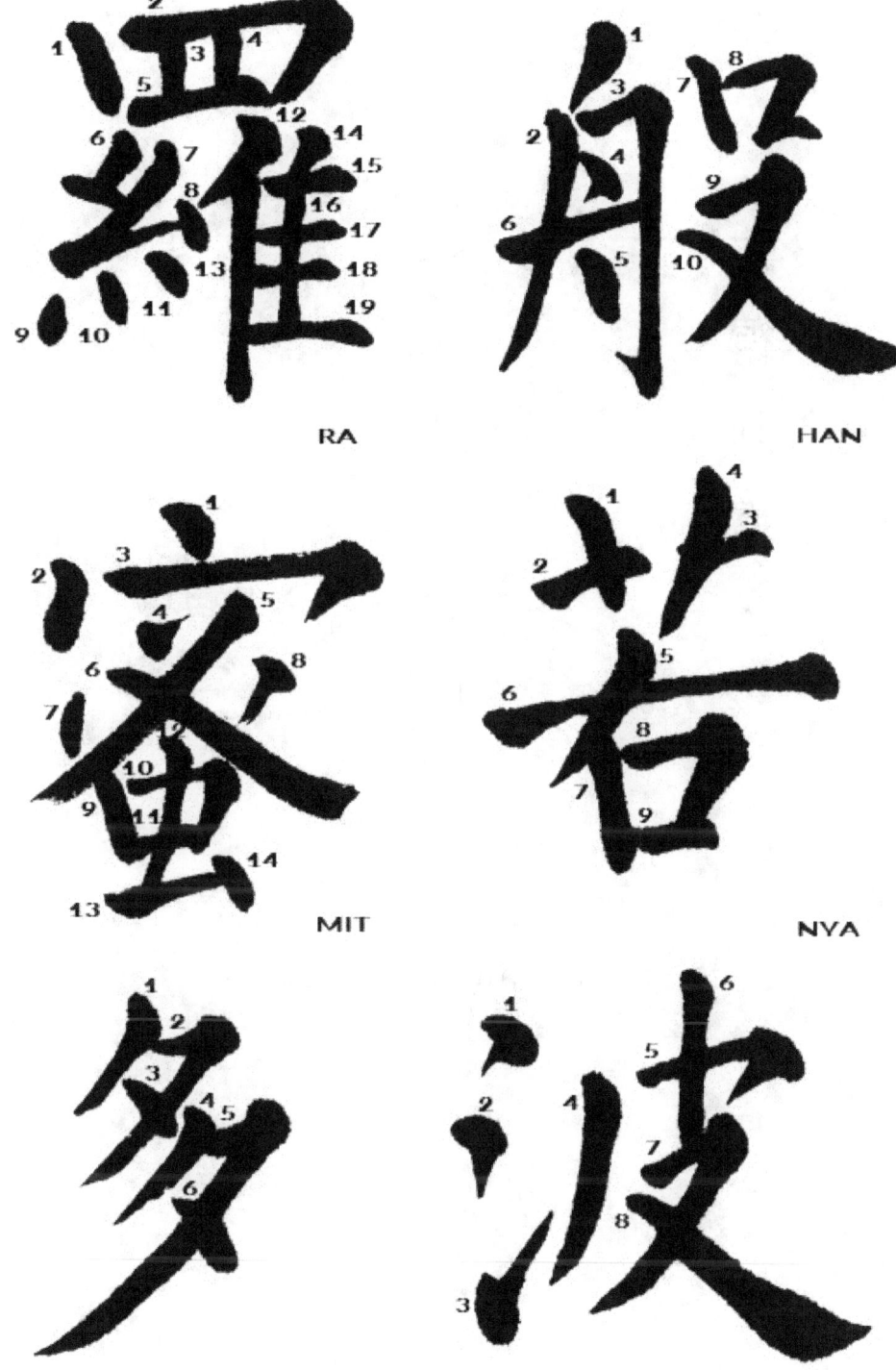

RA

HAN

MIT

NYA

TA

HA

故　KO　therefore

得　TOKU　attain

阿　A

耨　NOKU　annutara

多　TA

羅　RA

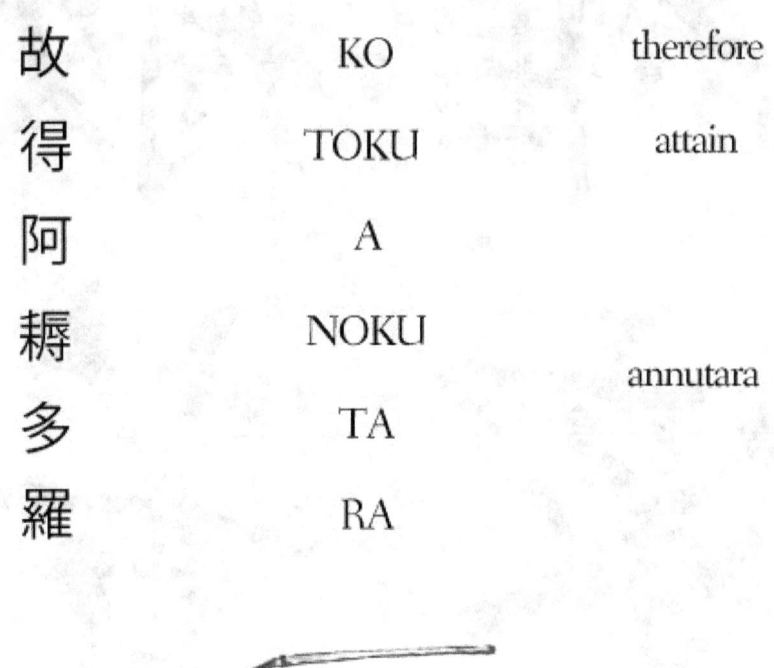

and thus awake to supreme,

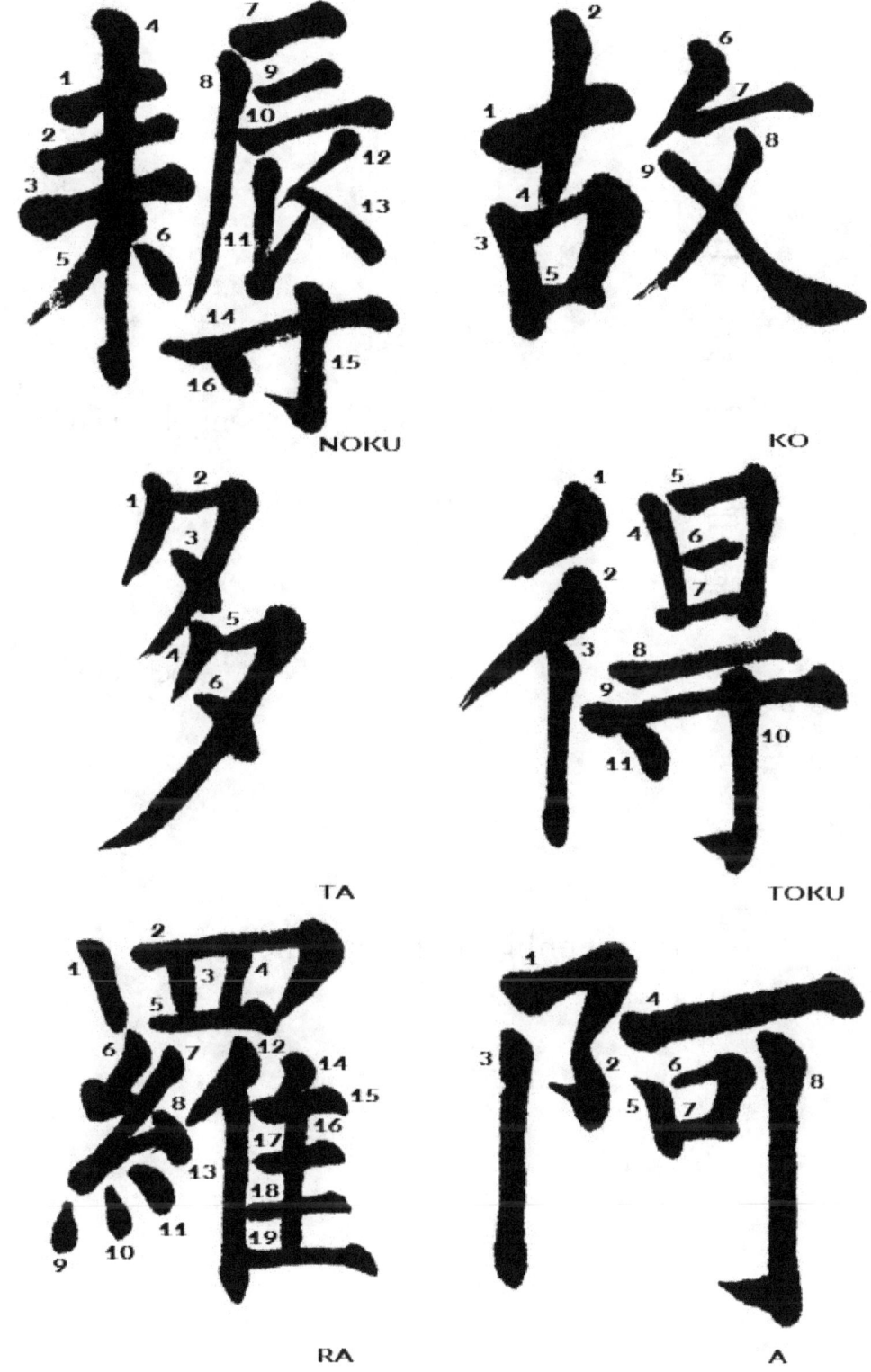

NOKU

KO

TA

TOKU

RA

A

三
藐
三
菩
提
故

SAN

MYAKU

SAN

BO

DAI

KO

samyaksambodhi

therefore

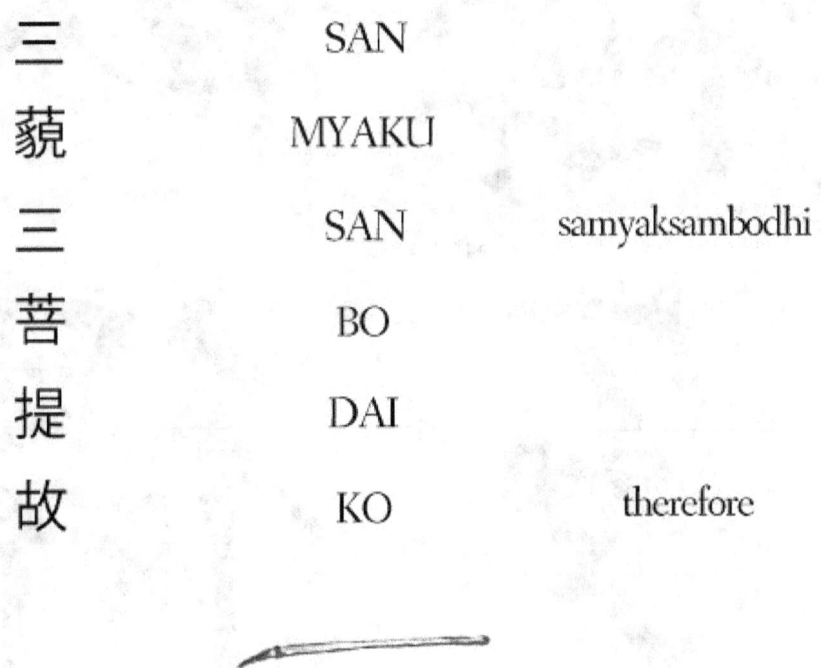

perfect enlightenment. Therefore

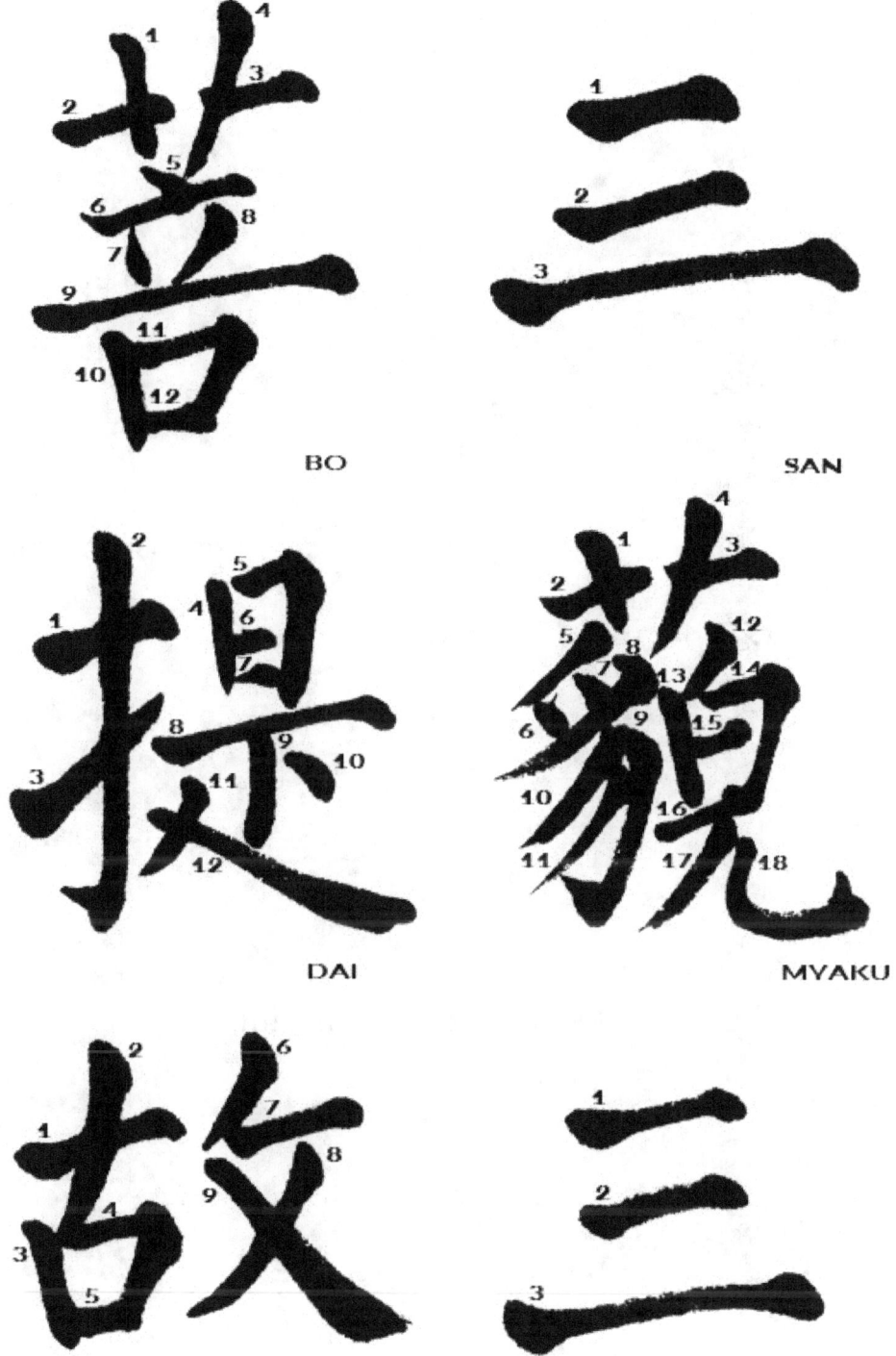

菩 BO

三 SAN

提 DAI

藐 MYAKU

故 KO

三 SAN

知　CHI　　　know

般　HAN

若　NYA

波　HA　　　prajnaparami(ta)

羅　RA

蜜　MIT

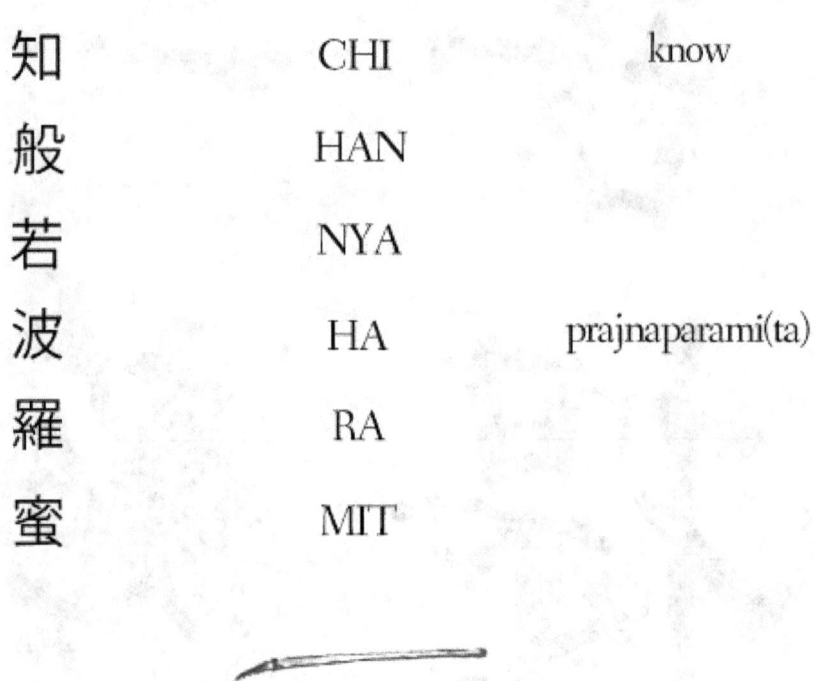

know Prajnaparamita

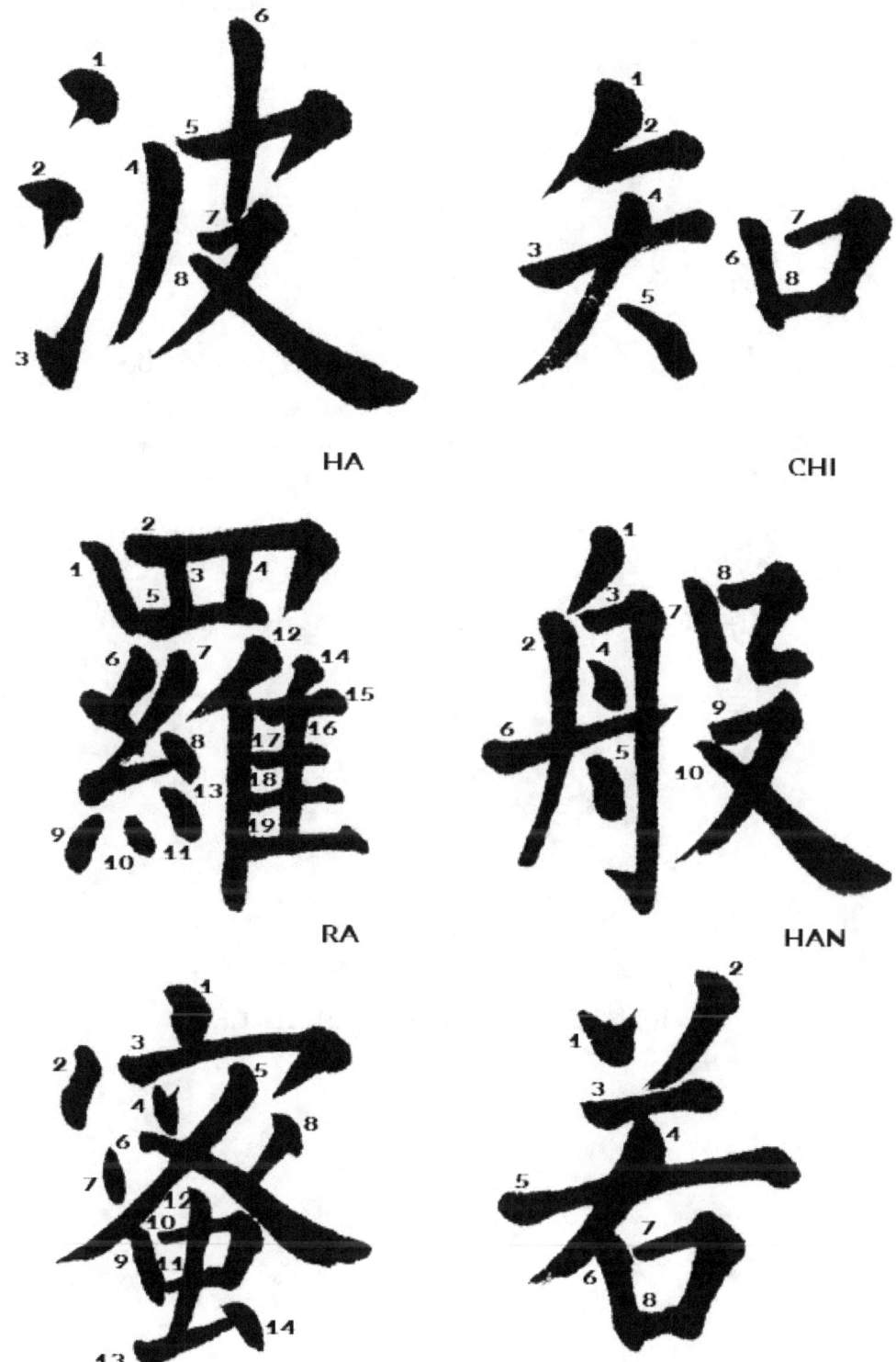

HA

CHI

RA

HAN

MIT

NYA

多
是
大
神
呪
是

TA	ta
ZE	be
DAI	great
JIN	spiritual
SHU	mantra
ZE	be

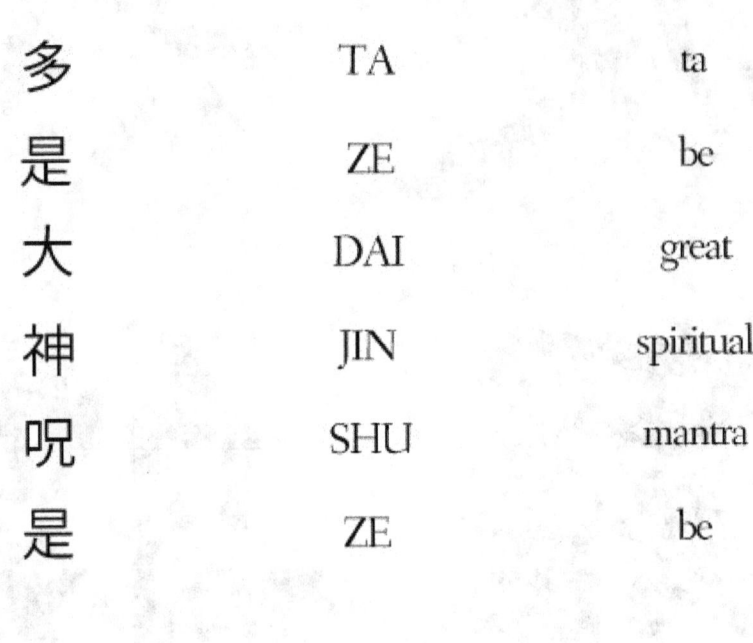

as the great spiritual mantra,

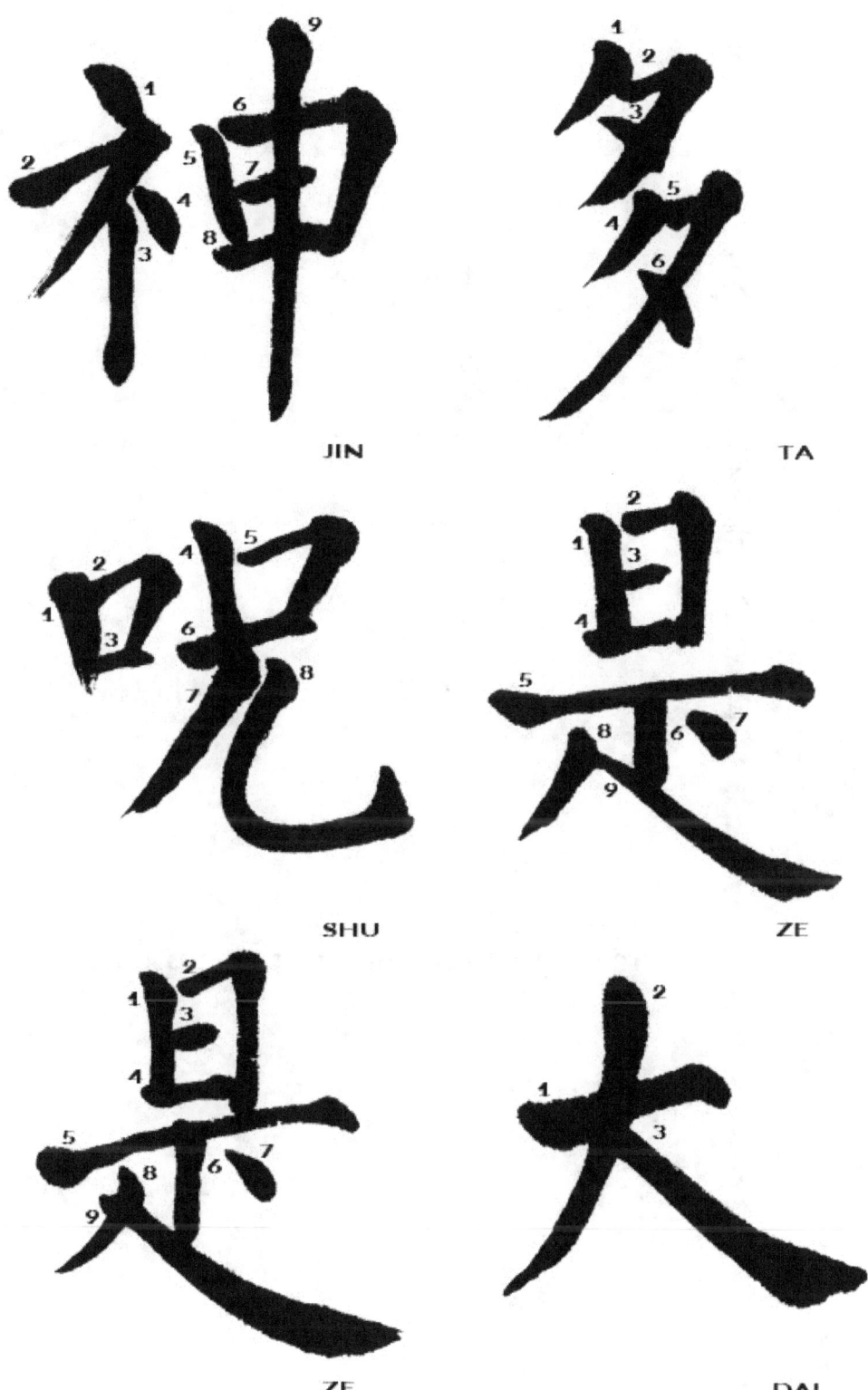

JIN

TA

SHU

ZE

ZE

DAI

大	DAI	great
明	MYŌ	knowledge
呪	SHU	mantra
是	ZE	be
無	MU	not
上	JŌ	higher

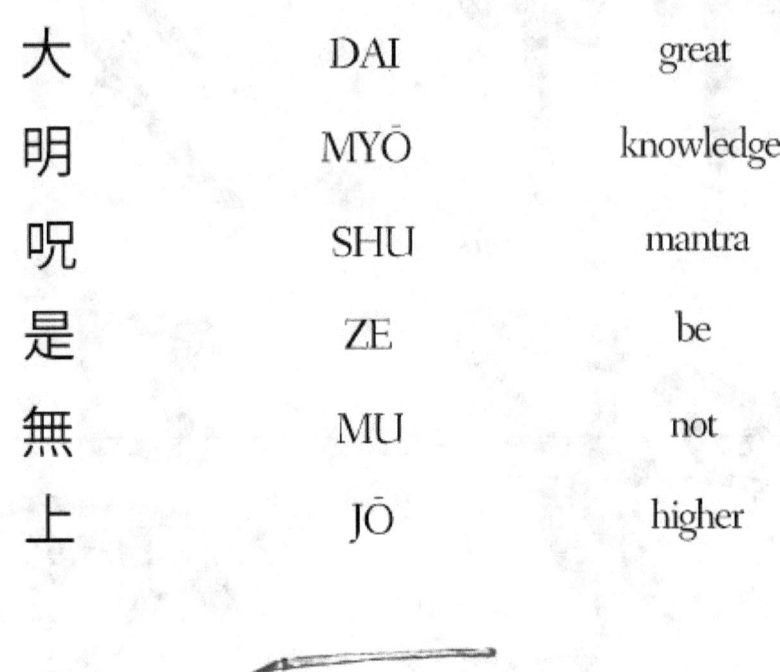

the mantra of great knowledge, the supreme

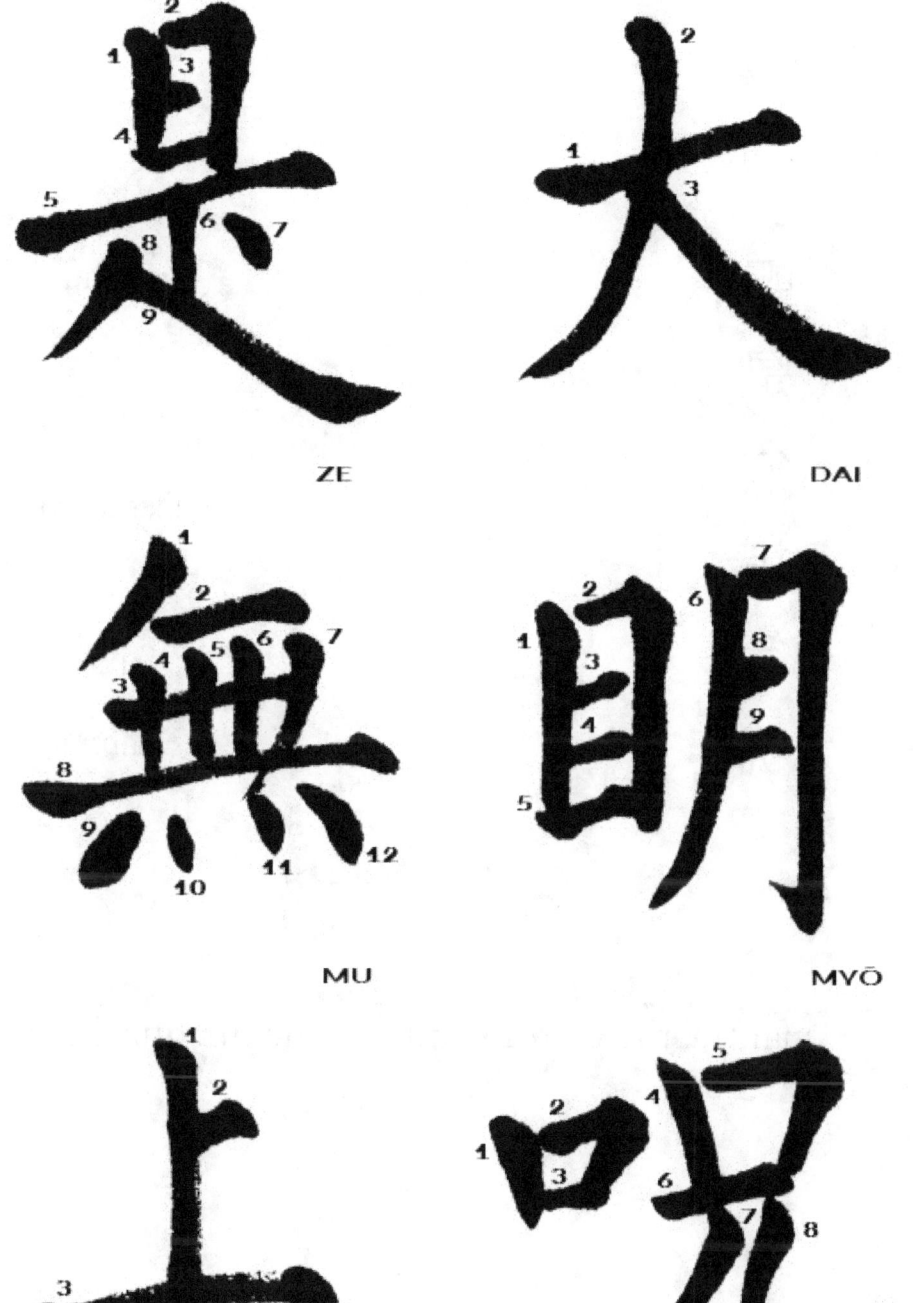

ZE

DAI

MU

MYŌ

JŌ

SHU

呪	SHU	mantra
是	ZE	be
無	MU	unequaled
等	TŌ	
等	DŌ	equal
呪	SHU	mantra

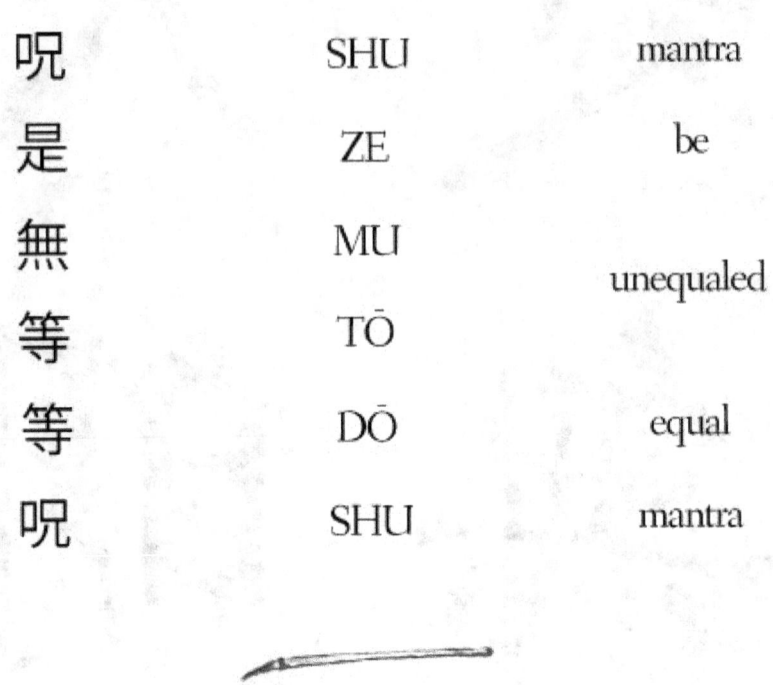

mantra, the mantra equal to the unequaled,

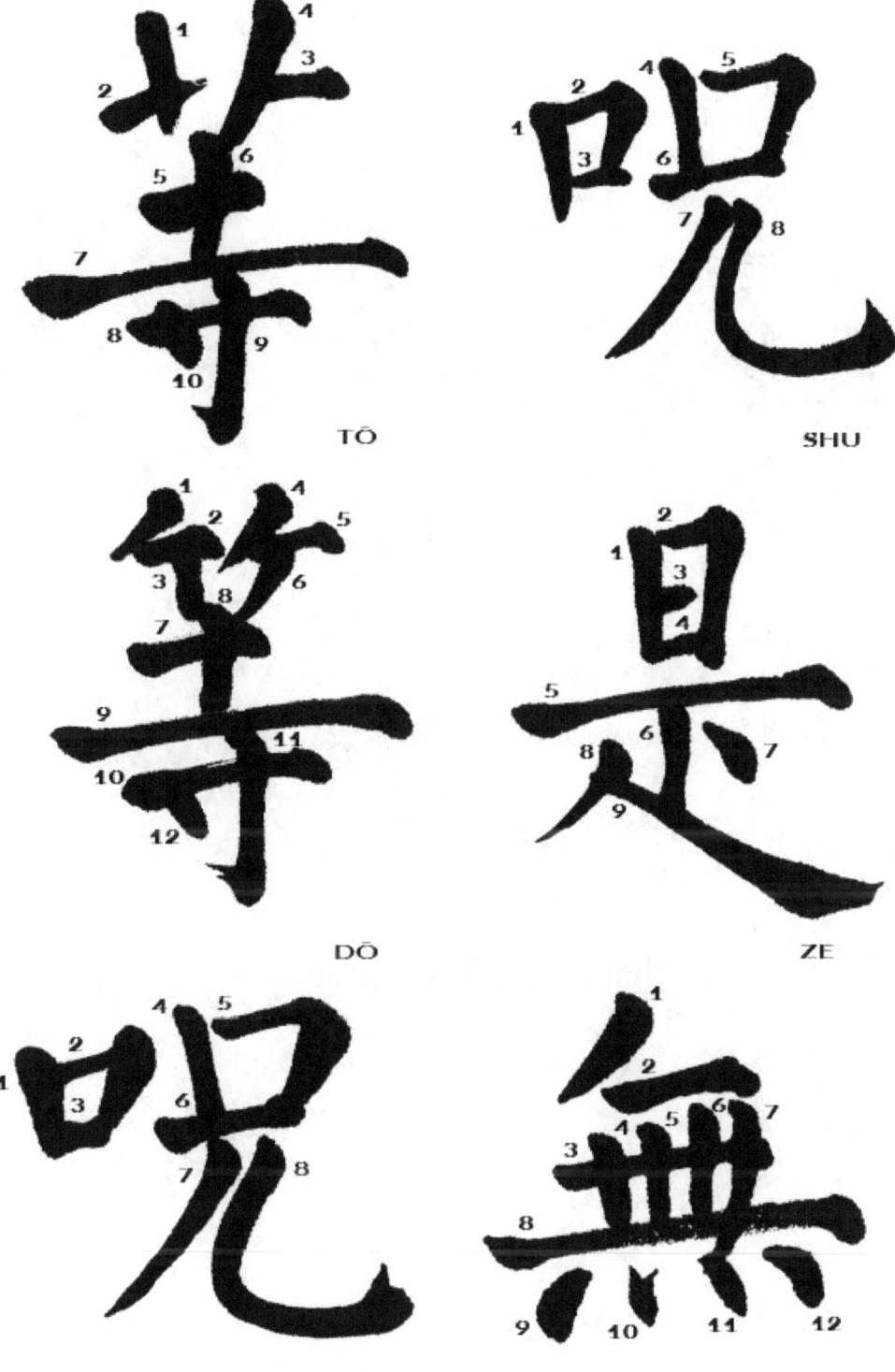

TŌ

SHU

DŌ

ZE

SHU

MU

能　NŌ　remove

除　JO

一　IS　all

切　SAI

苦　KU　suffering

真　SHIN　true

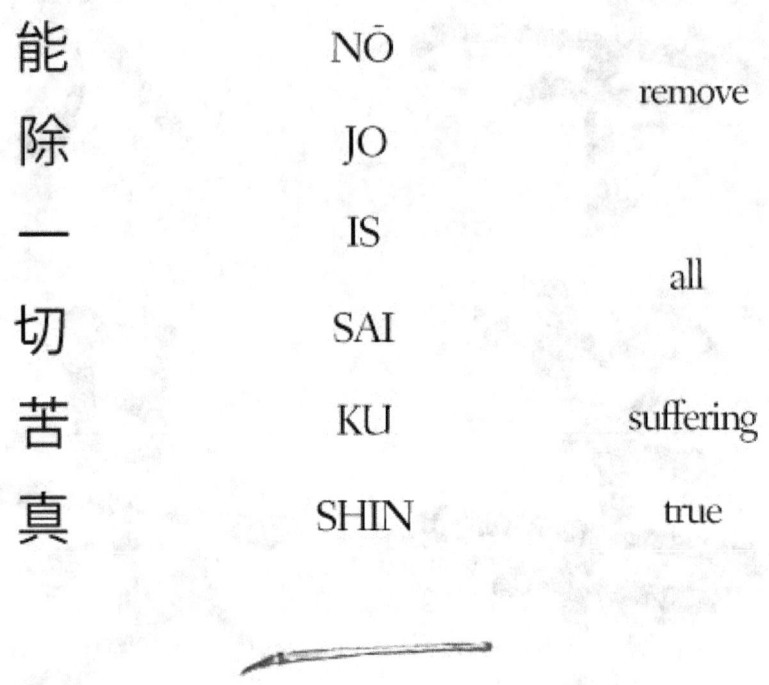

that heals all suffering, it is

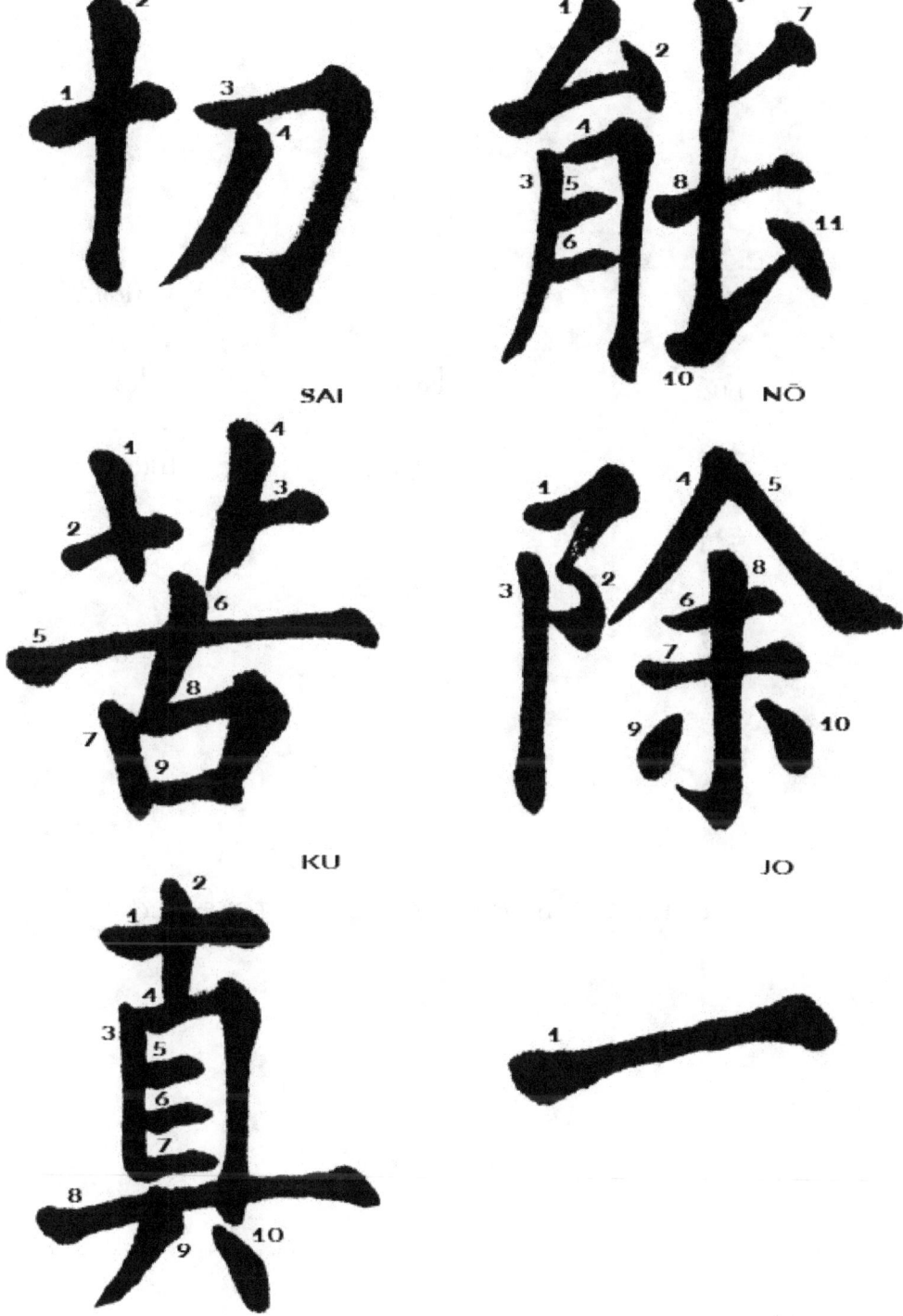

切 SAI

能 NŌ

苦 KU

除 JO

真 SHIN

一 IS

實	JITSU	true
不	FU	not
虛	KO	false
故	KO	therefore
説	SETSU	speak
般	HAN	praj

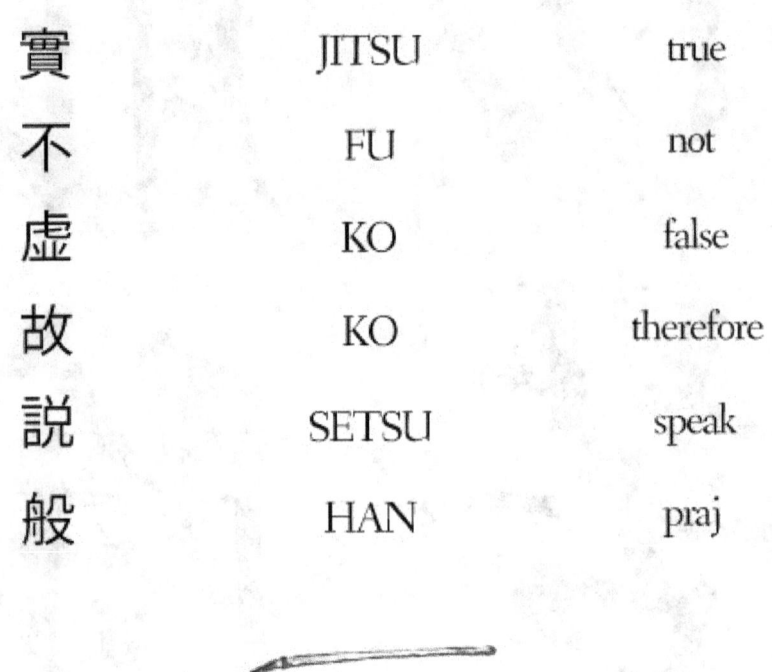

true, not false. The mantra revealed

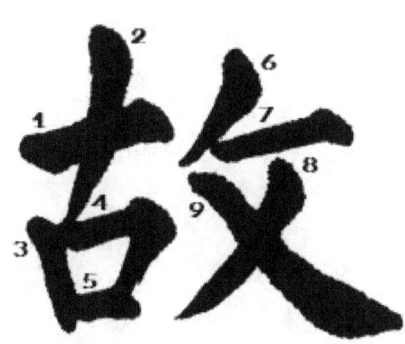

KO

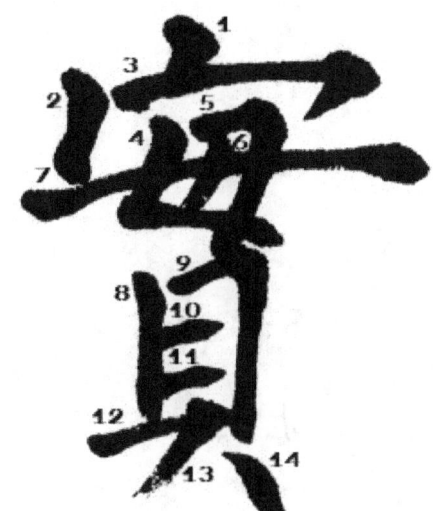

JITSU

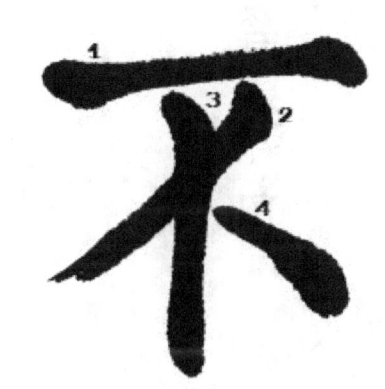

SETSU

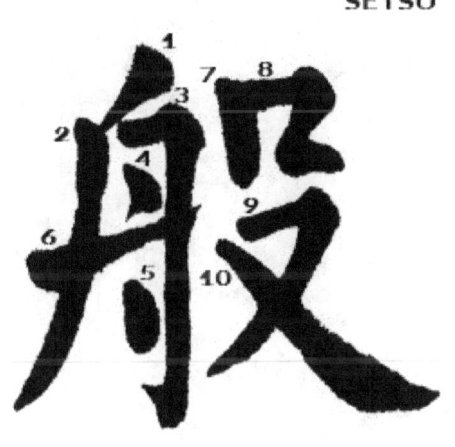

HAN

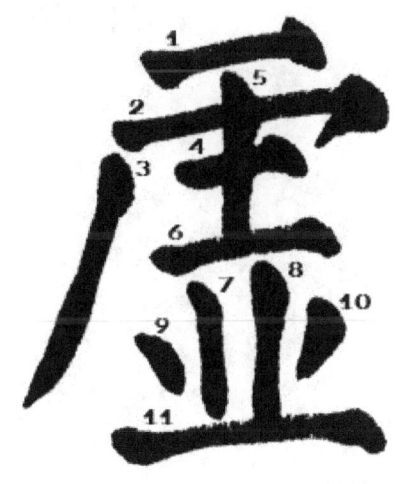

KO

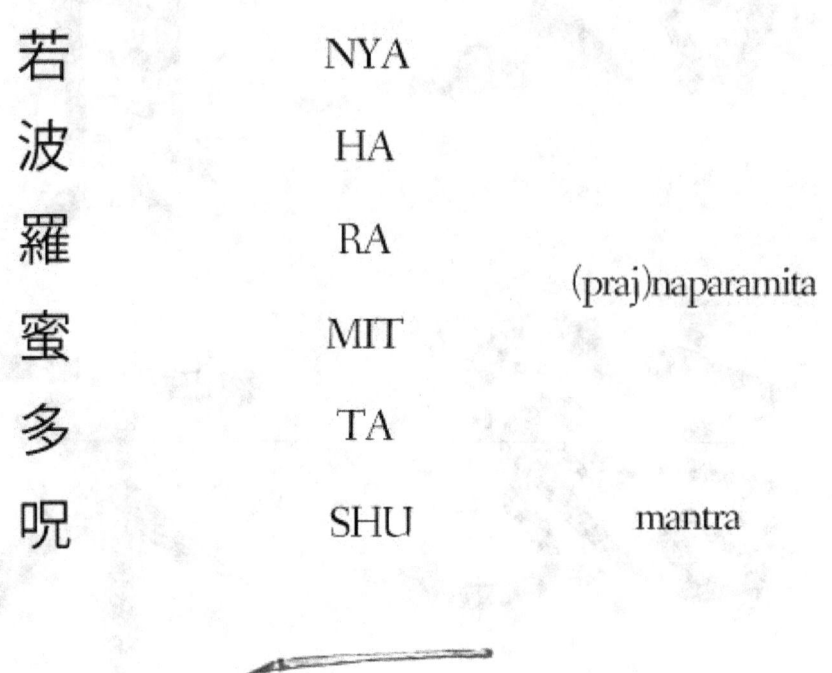

若　　NYA
波　　HA
羅　　RA
蜜　　MIT　　(praj)naparamita
多　　TA
呪　　SHU　　mantra

by Prajnaparamita

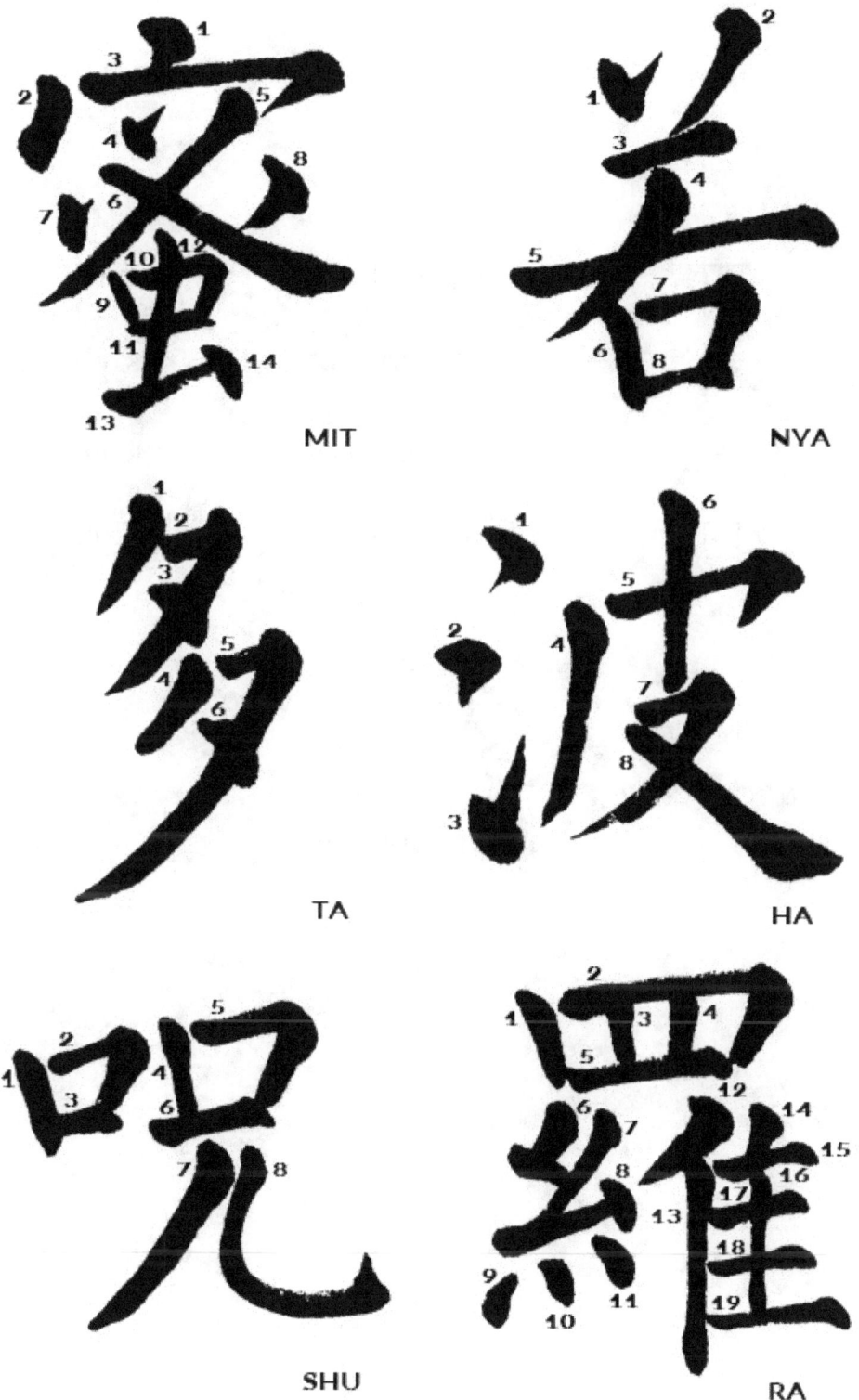

MIT

NYA

TA

HA

SHU

RA

即	SOKU	thus
説	SETSU	say
呪	SHU	mantra
曰	WATSU	speak

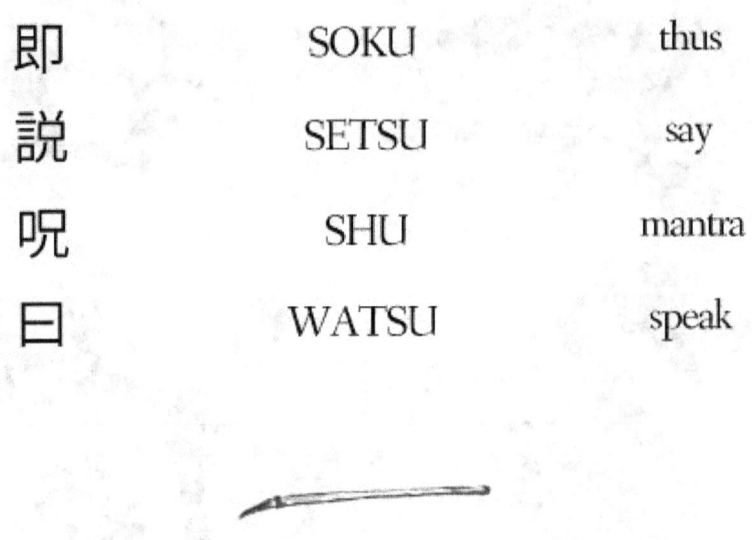

is spoken thus:

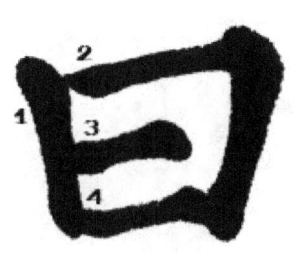

WATSU

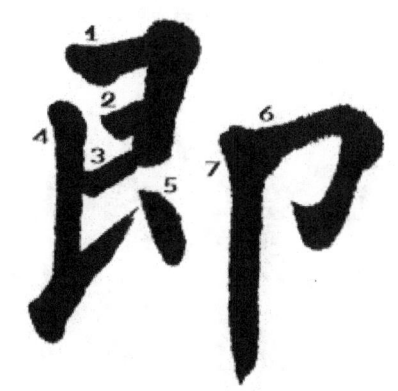

SOKU

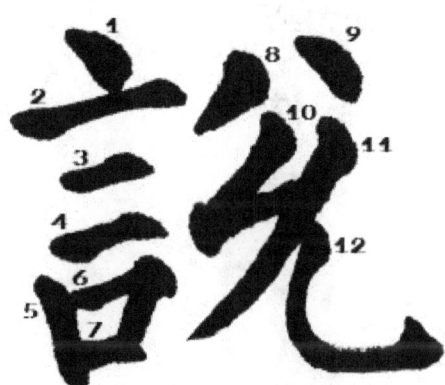

SETSU

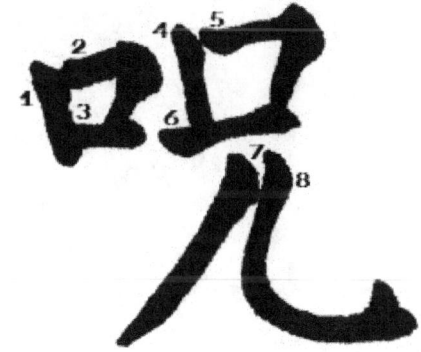

SHU

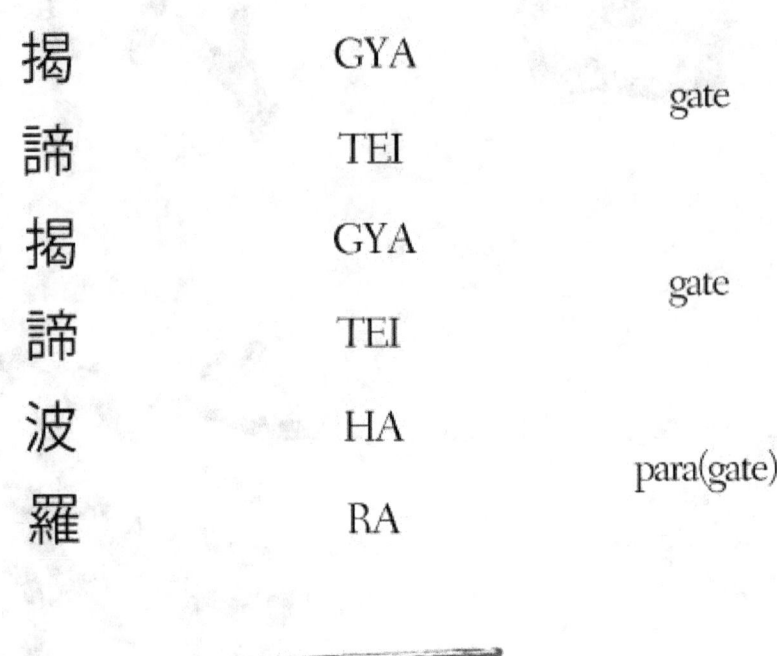

揭　GYA　gate

諦　TEI

揭　GYA　gate

諦　TEI

波　HA　para(gate)

羅　RA

"Gate gate, paragate,

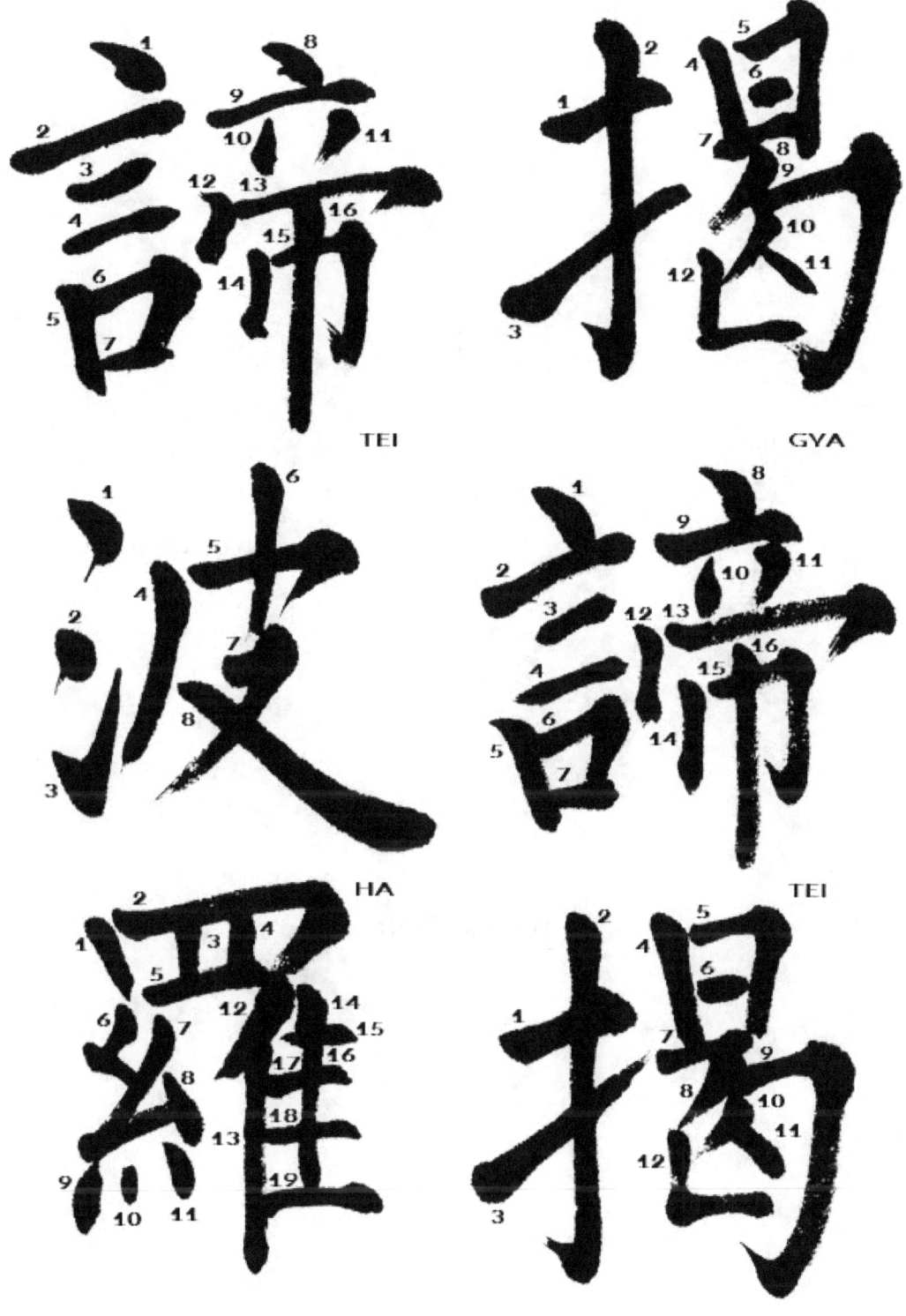

TEI

GYA

HA

TEI

RA

GYA

揭諦波羅僧揭

GYA
TEI
HA
RA
SŌ
GYA

gate

parasanga(te)

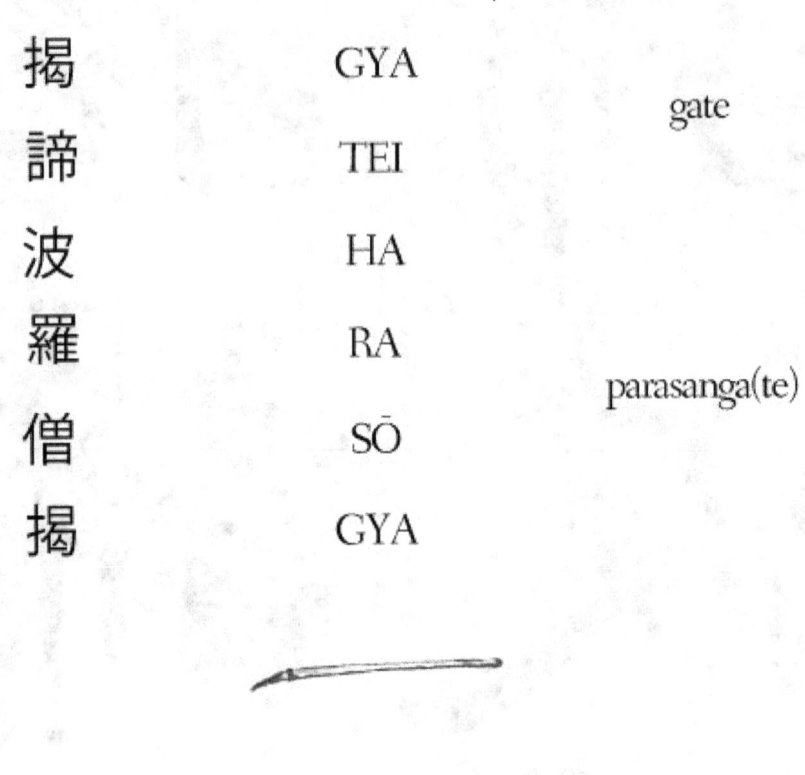

parasangate,

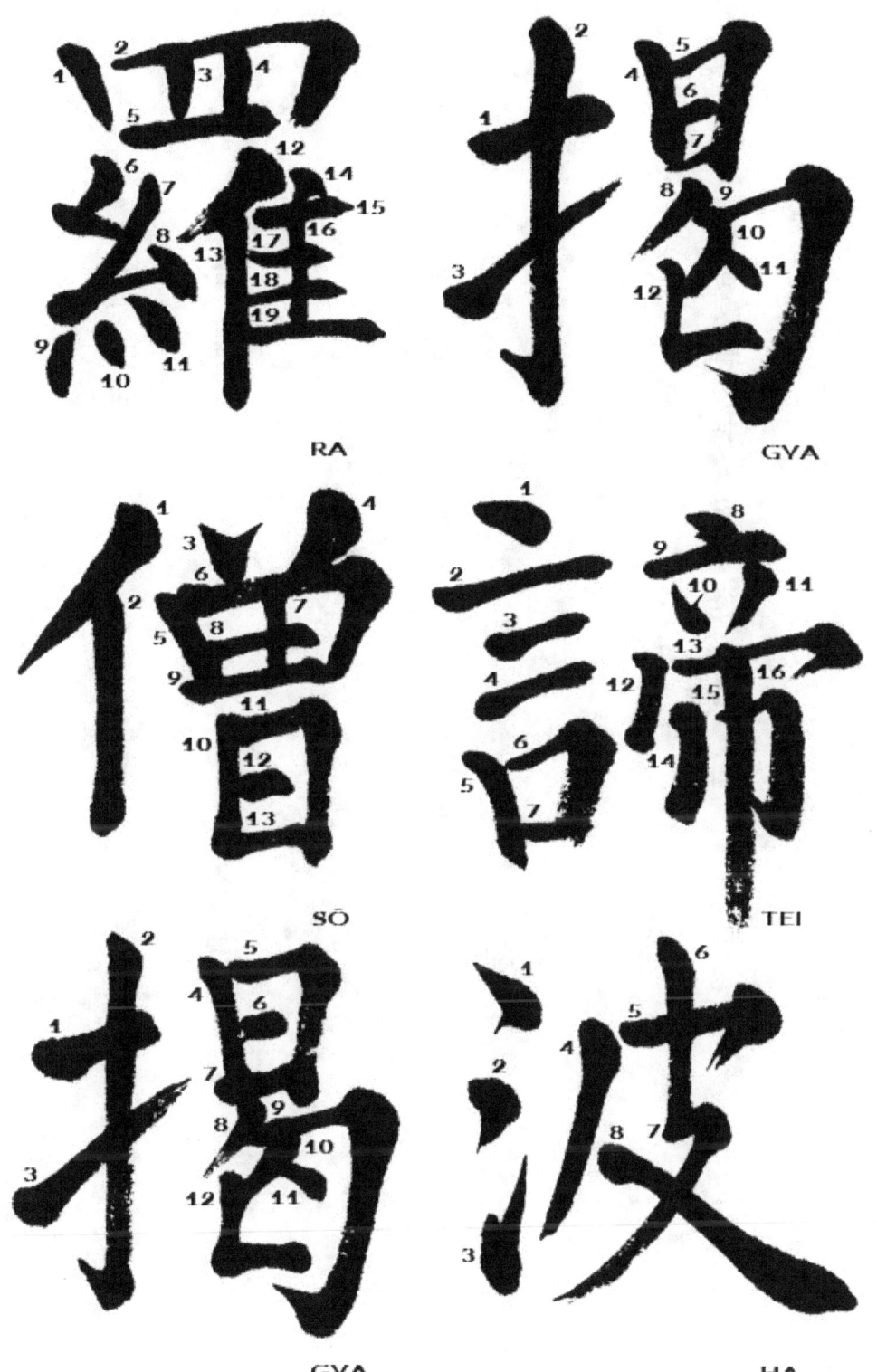

RA

GYA

SŌ

TEI

GYA

HA

諦　TEI　　　　te

菩　BO

提　JI　　　　bodhi

薩　SO

婆　WA　　　　svaha

訶　KA

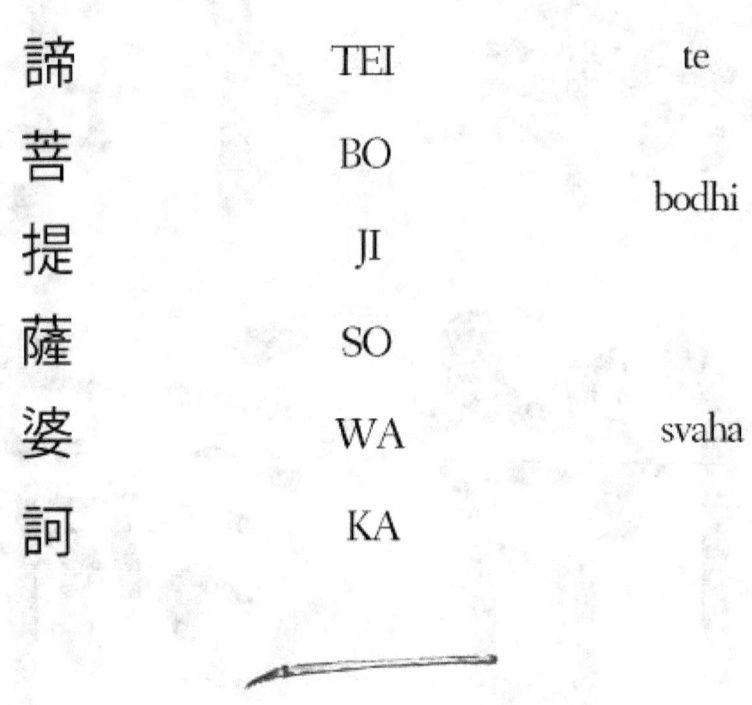

bodhi svaha".

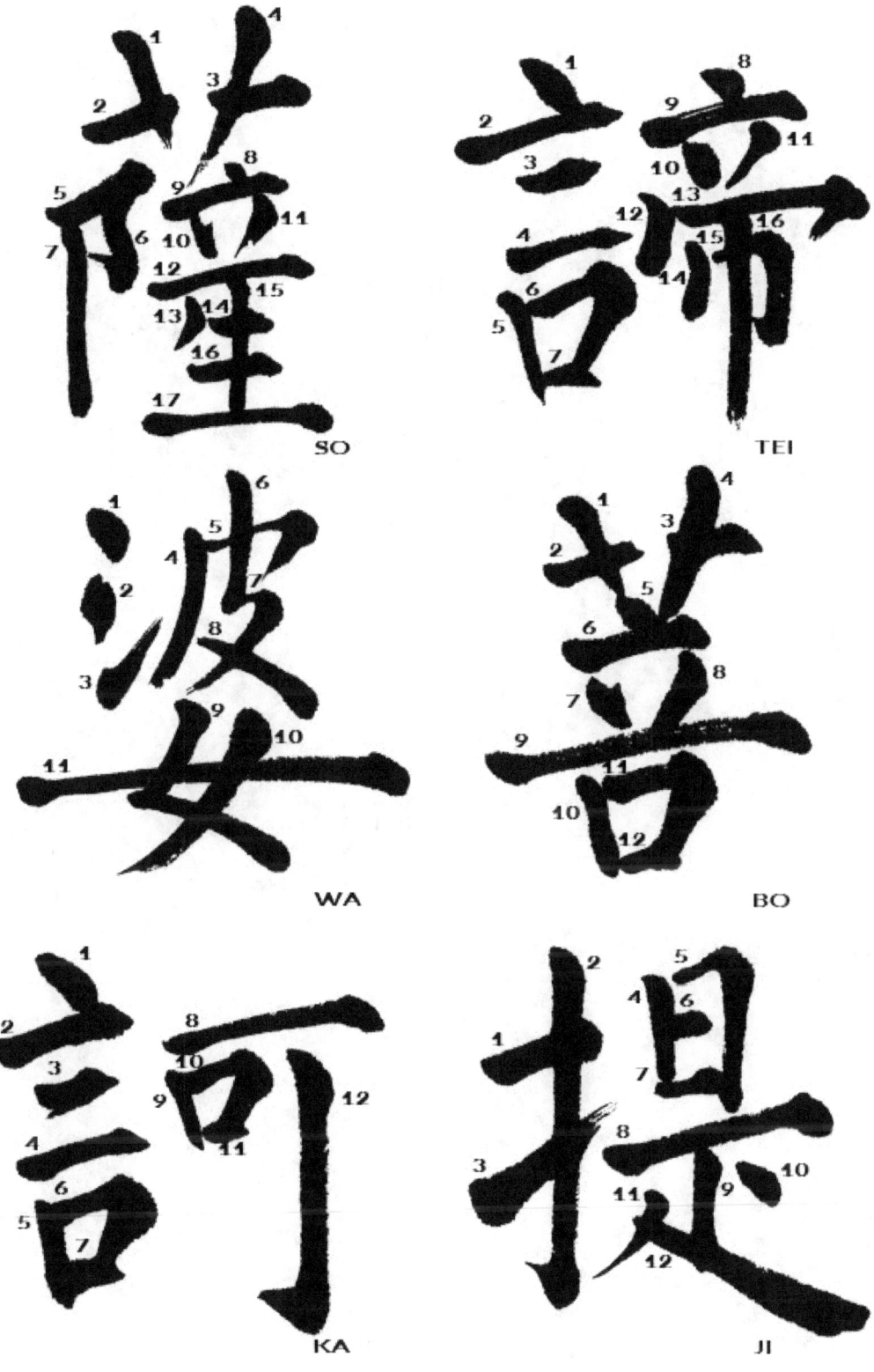

SO

TEI

WA

BO

KA

JI

般若心経

HAN   prajna

NYA

SHIN   heart

GYŌ   sutra

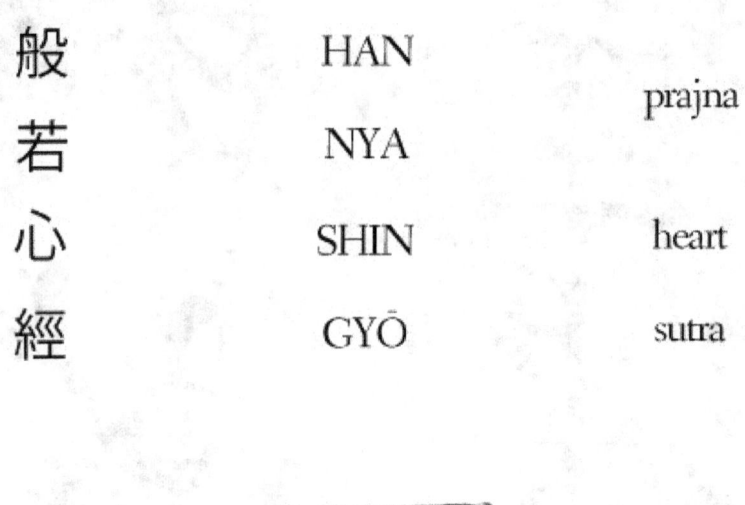

Prajna Heart Sutra.

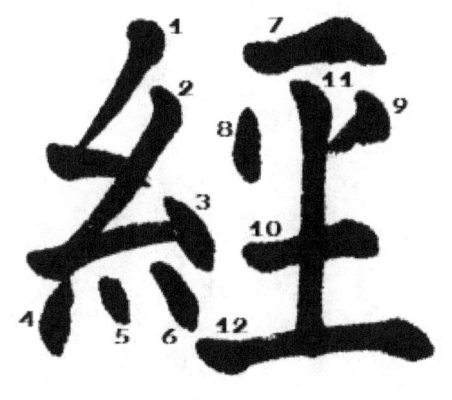

GYŌ

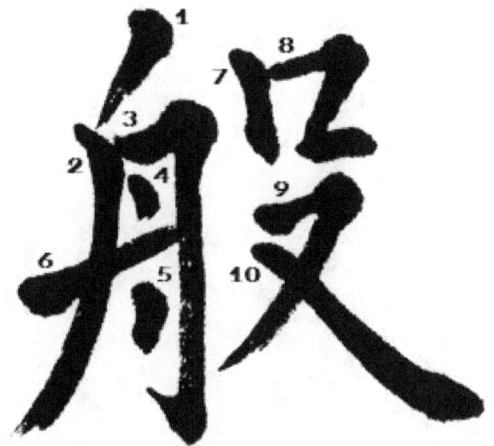

HAN

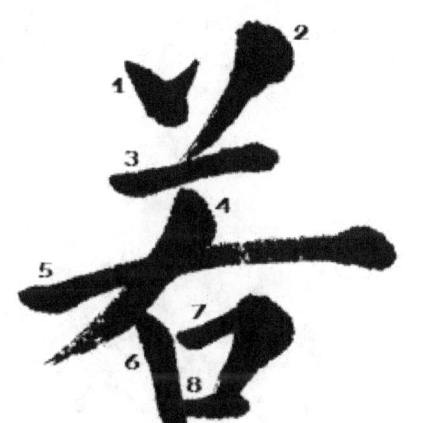

NYA

SHIN

Also by Nadja Van Ghelue

The Heart Sutra in Calligraphy: A Visual Appreciation of The Perfection of Wisdom

A compelling artistic copy of the Heart Sutra in seal script, brushed and introduced by the artist herself. A second edition is published by Echo Point Books & Media.

She has dedicated a large part of her Dharma and artistic life to the practice of copying the Heart Sutra. Much of her artwork is inspired by the Buddhist Prajnaparamita, the Perfection of Wisdom teachings. Please visit her online art gallery where she showcases her expressive Zen calligraphy and ink paintings.

https://www.theartofcalligraphy.com

You can read more about the many virtues of the practice of Heart Sutra copying at :

https://www.theartofcalligraphy.com/sutracopying

If you want to share your Heart Sutra copy visit this page:

https://www.theartofcalligraphy.com/share-your-heart-sutra-copying

www.ingramcontent.com/pod-product-compliance
Lightning Source LLC
Chambersburg PA
CBHW081733220526

45468CB00008B/2084